FROM MANGO
CUBA TO
PRICKLY PEAR
AMERICA

AN AMERICAN'S JOURNEY TO CASTRO'S CUBA AND BACK

FROM MANGO CUBA TO PRICKLY PEAR AMERICA

AN AMERICAN'S JOURNEY TO CASTRO'S CUBA AND BACK

MELINDA VOSS

FROM MANGO CUBA TO PRICKLY PEAR AMERICA
AN AMERICAN'S JOURNEY TO CASTRO'S CUBA AND BACK

iUniverse books may be ordered through booksellers or by contacting:

iUniverse
1663 Liberty Drive
Bloomington, IN 47403
www.iuniverse.com
1-800-Authors (1-800-288-4677)

Because of the dynamic nature of the Internet, any web addresses or links contained in this book may have changed since publication and may no longer be valid. The views expressed in this work are solely those of the author and do not necessarily reflect the views of the publisher, and the publisher hereby disclaims any responsibility for them.

Any people depicted in stock imagery provided by Thinkstock are models, and such images are being used for illustrative purposes only.
Certain stock imagery © Thinkstock.

ISBN: 978-1-5320-3409-1 (sc)
ISBN: 978-1-5320-3408-4 (e)

Library of Congress Control Number: 2017919275

Print information available on the last page.

iUniverse rev. date: 03/27/2018

CONTENTS

To the Cuban people, for their tireless resilience, relentless exuberance in the face of adversity, and untold contributions to the world

Mango: 1) a yellow-red, oblong tropical fruit loved by the Cuban people; 2) a colloquial expression in Cuba used to describe something desirable, such as a hot, sexy guy.

PREFACE

Before stepping on the airplane to Havana in March 2014, I had to confront myself. Was I going as a curious tourist or an inquiring journalist? I knew I would view everything in Cuba through the eyes of a reporter. I knew it would make me crazy not to ask questions and take notes. But I didn't want to do all that work. Wouldn't it be easier to simply enjoy myself? In the end, I gave in to my journalistic impulse. I simply had to make sense of what I saw—for myself, if for no one else. At the same time, I recognized that I was presumptuous to assume I could spend a week in Cuba and write a meaningful e-book about a country, its people, and my experiences. After all, we were shepherded around the island on a tightly controlled schedule and kept within sight of government employees most of the touring time.

Why would I dare to do such a thing? Though not an expert in anything Cuban, I am a practiced observer of people, situations, and life from twenty-six years as a newspaper reporter and as a longtime student of human behavior. I have learned to spot salient details and facts; record, analyze, and articulate them; and, above all, question, question, question. Indeed, I question everything, especially my own motives, opinions, and prejudices.

The result is this volume in which I seek to provide a thoughtful glimpse of what life is like for ordinary Cubans and a window into understanding the Cuban character and myself, for that matter. Also, I was curious to juxtapose what I saw in Cuba with what exists in the United States. The comparisons and contrasts seem striking. My perspective and conclusions were molded by firsthand observations, conversations with Cubans and Americans, research, and reflection. It wasn't until I returned from Cuba that I conducted the research providing critical background for my views. I drew on an extensive array of credible sources to provide a historical and sociological context that I hadn't picked up in my weeklong trip. In fact, I verified pretty much everything our Cuban guide told us on sites that I trust, such as the World Bank, the CIA Book of Facts, and other credible sources.

Despite a stunted economy, Cuba offers a treasure trove of historical sites, entertainment, and natural beauty for tourists. It would be easy to focus only on the tourist attractions. But that's not my purpose here. There are plenty of guidebooks for that. This book is designed as a primer for people who want an overview view—a context—in which to think about this fascinating country and its relationship to America. I also share what I learned about myself and my misshapen views of Cuba before I went. Some of the lessons were a rude awakening. But then travel is broadening if you want it to be, isn't it? The journey just didn't broaden me in ways I had expected.

This book is laid out roughly in the chronological order of the tour, with bits woven throughout about Cuba's history, customs, housing, education system, agriculture, health care, family life, and aging, among other topics. I concentrated on what surprised and interested me and on what I thought Americans should know. During my visit, we covered a lot of ground. We toured the stately University of Havana; visited the Santeria Cultural Center, Che Guevara's tomb, Revolution Square, a tobacco farm, and an organic farm; and learned about community projects focused on neighborhood revitalization, young people with Down syndrome, and senior citizens. We experienced an impressive array of Cuban musicians and artists, including a live performance of the well-known Buena Vista Social Club and the mind-boggling work by Jose Rodrigues Fuster, known as the Picasso of the Caribbean.

While I do not pretend that we saw a complete picture of Cuban life or always heard unbiased information, our guide took all questions and showed as much as she told, allowing us to judge a lot for ourselves. I talked to other Cubans along the way but have left out most of their names, as I'm uncertain whether they would face repercussions from anything they said. In some cases, I found them to be unusually frank.

Our two New World countries share so much. We have a tangled and troubled history, common racial and ethnic injustices past and present, and cultures embraced enthusiastically by both peoples. Perhaps because of my long-standing fascination with our island neighbor, I also wanted to understand the role that United States and American citizens played in Cuba's history. In short, how did US interventions help or hurt the Cuban people?

Until researching for this book, I had mostly a schoolgirl's understanding of US actions. Of course, I knew how William Randolph Hearst and other Americans goaded the US government into the Spanish-American War. I knew about varying accounts of Teddy Roosevelt's ventures in Cuba during the Spanish-American War. I knew Havana was a hot spot for gamblers, mobsters, and movie stars in the thirties, forties, and fifties. And I knew that Fidel Castro was a leader who held down his people with brute force and executions but who also struck a blow for Cuban pride.

What I discovered about Cuba and the United States is heartening and discouraging at the same time. Since then, Fidel Castro died on November 25, 2016, at age ninety. Donald Trump, who declared he would put America first, was elected president of the United States. The implications of these two events have yet to play out. Will Fidel's passing mark the beginning of a new era? We'll see. Regardless, he remains a fascinating though deeply flawed figure who made a powerful impact—for good and for ill—on his country, the United States, and the world. Will Trump continue the hard-line Republican view against embracing Cuba? Or will he give in to his moneymaking impulses and open up Cuba?

Given all this, I seek to build appreciation, connection, and a mutually beneficial relationship with America's neighbor. If more Americans without ties to Cuba visit this island and experience its wonders, more political support will build for lifting the outdated and failed embargo. Bipartisan support in Congress is building. The entire Minnesota congressional delegation, which includes three Republicans, supports lifting the embargo.

I urge Americans to visit Cuba. With Cuba and the United States restoring diplomatic relations, the stage is set for a new friendship and productive relationship for both countries. See and judge for yourself. To that end, I humbly offer *Mango Cuba and Prickly Pear America: An American's Journey to Castro's Cuba and Back* as an aid. I welcome all feedback.

CHAPTER 1

Anticipation

My sleep was fitful in the early-morning hours of March 10, 2014. I was at a Miami hotel, having traveled the day before from my home in Saint Paul, Minnesota. When the wake-up call came at a quarter after four, I arose with a queasy stomach but also a profound sense of relief and anticipation. My body knew something big was ahead.

I was about to set foot in Cuba, a country that had fascinated me since I was a little girl. Born in 1950, I grew up amid dinner table conversations about the Cuban revolution, which began in 1953, and its aftermath. I was nine years old in January 1959 when Fidel and Raúl Castro toppled the dictator, Fulgencio Batista, and ushered Communism in under the approving eye of the Soviet Union. Now I was about to head to the Miami airport with thirty-one other Americans on a people-to-people visa to explore Cuba's complexity, its leaders, its people, its culture, and its relationship with America.

During the forty-five-minute flight across the Caribbean Sea, I could barely see the swells and the whitecaps. The dark blue waters reflected the partly sunny, partly cloudy sky. The weather was emblematic of my mixed feelings about Cuba. The sunny part drew warm memories of watching the Cuban American actor Desi Arnaz play Ricky Ricardo in my favorite TV show of the fifties, *I Love Lucy*. The clouds created shadows that seemed reminiscent of the overloaded boats of hopeful Cubans who drowned trying to reach America. Looking back from my vantage point in 2017 on those first moments in the air above Havana, it seems almost impossible to believe that we have come so far and yet have so far to go.

The plane descended fast. The wheels bumped onto the tarmac. When the cabin door opened, the first wave of tropical humidity swept over me. My heartbeat quickened as I exited the plane. I knew I'd never be quite the same when I returned to the Midwest, a land of countless cornfields instead of swaying palms.

Approaching Cuban customs, I thought of a morning in 1962 when I was walking to church with my father. He had explained in a somber voice that war could break out at any moment. Hearing that the Soviets had smuggled missiles into Cuba, I felt afraid then. A few days later, the Soviets agreed to remove their missiles. The threat was over. I resumed my life as a prepubescent girl thinking about my hairstyle and the rock 'n' roll sensation of the time, the Beatles.

Now arriving in Havana fifty-two years later, I had no fear. Instead, my thoughts began vacillating between impatience with America's refusal to lift the trade embargo and recognition that the Cuban government has killed and imprisoned dissidents, swept aside human rights, stunted its economy, and stifled free speech. I was eager to learn about Cuba and its people. I had dozens of questions: What were the Cuban people like? What challenges did they confront on a daily basis? What did Cubans think of Americans? How had Cuba changed since the fifties? Would we ever get back to full diplomatic relations and be able to travel freely in each other's country? What could Americans learn from Cubans?

Those questions were quickly swept aside when we met our Cuban guide, Nilda Elena Fuentes Diaz, at the airport. Greeting us with a large smile and a jaunty manner, she captivated me immediately. Her palpable energy felt as delightful and embracing as the tropical sun did after leaving Minnesota's bitter cold.

Nilda was an impressive representative of the Cuban people. She had earned a degree in French from the University of Havana, Cuba's most prestigious university. Her English was impeccable—no grammatical errors, hardly a mispronounced word, and an enviable vocabulary. Poised and articulate, she spiced informative talks with humor, personal anecdotes, and a reminder that the ubiquitous rum-laced "welcome cocktail" would greet us at nearly every stop.

With golden-honey skin, she had the look of Spanish descent. Large black eyes matched her shiny dark hair, which flowed past her shoulders, though she usually pulled it into a ponytail. About five feet five and less than 110 pounds, her slender frame barely filled her uniform, which consisted of a navy sweater, a short-sleeved white blouse with navy-blue trim, and navy slacks or a pencil skirt. She was married then with no children. In 2015, she had a baby girl. I was thrilled for her.

Like most Cubans, Nilda worked for the government. Then age twenty-eight, she embodied, for me, the hope of a new generation of Cubans. Indeed, the Cubans we met smiled and laughed often. They certainly didn't look downtrodden. Pride in their country and its heritage was evident. Their bodies moved with grace and confidence. They spoke often of a better future.

Back then, they had reason to be hopeful. Just a few years before, President Raúl Castro had eased more than three hundred economic restrictions on property use, travel, farming, municipal governance, electronics access, and more. Maybe I wanted to feel optimistic, but it seemed even then—just months before the December 2014 announcement that our two countries would reestablish diplomatic ties—that a new relationship had begun gestating.

Since then, I have been jolted by two events: President Obama's abrupt repeal of the longstanding "wet foot–dry foot" policy before he left office and the election of Donald Trump, who has vowed to take a hard-line approach with Cuba. Under the new policy, Cubans who arrive in the United States without visas will be classified as undocumented immigrants instead of being granted a right to stay in the United States and on a fast track to citizenship.

Once again, Cubans must feel like pawns of the US government, a situation that has been playing out since the 1880s, when Americans began investing in Cuba's then prosperous sugar and tobacco plantations. The reaction of Cuban officials is yet to be determined, but I'm not placing any bets on Trump improving relations with Cuba. The Cubans have played Americans for fools before. The question is, With Raúl Castro set to step down in 2018 as president, will the old guard, as represented by the late Fidel Castro and his brother, give way to a more progressive leader with a friendlier attitude toward the United States?

But in 2014, those events were yet to play out.

During my weeklong tour of Cuba, Nilda led us through packed itineraries every day from eight in the morning to nine o'clock at night. Each morning, we set out in our sleek, air-conditioned tour bus with cushioned seats and comfortable headrests. We sat high above people on the street. Often, I felt like a voyeur who could form judgments based on nothing more than a passing glance. Each night, I collapsed in a high-quality hotel, knowing these places were out of reach for most Cubans. At times, I wondered, why had I really come? Would we get a true picture of their lives or a varnished government view?

Yankee Savvy

One thing I know—Americans can be assured they will be welcomed in Cuba. I never felt a whiff of resentment or anger from any Cubans at how the United States and US business interests had treated, or should I say, mistreated the Cuban people. America may have turned its back on Cubans, but Cubans have not turned their backs on Americans.

Since President Obama began loosening restrictions on Americans traveling to Cuba, Americans have been flocking to Cuba. I saw my fellow citizens everywhere. Some are Cuban Americans who visit relatives. By 2016, the Cuban Ministry of Tourism estimated about six hundred thousand Americans, up 34 percent from the previous year, had visited the island, according to the *New York Times*. To obtain a visa to Cuba, Americans cannot simply go as tourists. They must declare one of twelve allowable reasons, which include humanitarian, religious, or educational activities, for the trip.

Cubans seemed intensely interested in Americans, and they understand a lot more about American culture than I had expected. For example, Nilda told us she was a huge fan of *Sex and the City*, the television comedy that ran from 1998 to 2004 about the lives of four young women in New York City. However, she noted that Cuban censors blocked the *Sex and the City* episode in which Mr. Big paints a wall red. Did the censors somehow think that conveyed an anti-Communist message? Flash drives and DVDs of American television shows and movies are routinely passed among friends and family to keep Cubans abreast of American trends.

First Awakenings

On the way from the airport to the famed Hotel Nacional de Cuba where we would stay, the tour bus stopped at the Plaza de la Revolución or Revolution Square. From the early days of Fidel Castro's rise in 1959, this is where thousands of Cubans gathered to hear his fiery speeches that went on for hours. A vast area of seventy-two thousand square meters, the square is reportedly one of the largest in the world. As the wind whipped through the wide-open space, my eyes were drawn to the star-shaped stone obelisk. It loomed large. At 350 feet high, it is a memorial to Jose Marti, a national hero of the Cuban revolution in the 1890s. Across the square on the side of a building, an iron sculpture outlines the likeness of Che Guevara, Castro's compatriot who helped him seize power. It was simple and understated.

Despite its place in history, the square seemed unpretentious and ordinary to me. The spot didn't particularly evoke any strong emotion. More recently, I was moved by the thousands of Cubans who gathered there in November 2016 to honor Fidel Castro after he died. They filed past a black-and-white picture of "El Comandante" as a young revolutionary carrying a rifle. Public Radio International reported that many Cubans "walked by silently, clutching flowers, some took pictures with their phones and others sobbed uncontrollably as they looked up at the portrait flanked by white roses."

After my visit to Revolution Square, we proceeded to the hotel, a historic symbol of Cuban and American history. We had a lunch of smoked salmon, beef, rice, and potatoes at a room specially set up for our group. Built in 1930, the hotel has a grand scale with 457 rooms, fifteen suites, and a presidential suite. The decor is understated but eloquent and somewhat frayed around the edges. Lots of dark wood gives it a rather formal feel. Framed black-and-white photos of US celebrities who stayed there, such as Frank Sinatra, Ava Gardner, Rita Hayworth, Rocky Marciano, Tyrone Power, Johnny Weismuller, and Gary Cooper, lend a charm and enticement for Americans, at least those of my vintage. It's easy to envision Marlon Brando in his *Godfather* role walking down a hallway. I felt thrilled and privileged to be there. Somehow, this kind of eloquence wasn't what I expected. Suddenly, a new view of Cuba began to emerge.

At our next stop, the University of Havana, I discovered that I had come to Cuba with a decidedly simplistic view. I had seen Cuba as unsophisticated and backward presumably because it had been cut off from America. In my narrow view, that meant they were cut off from everywhere else, too. Moreover, I realized, to my chagrin, that I hadn't known or thought much about Cuba's history *before* Castro.

I hadn't paid much attention to the fact that Cuba originally was inhabited by indigenous tribes. Once Christopher Columbus landed in 1492, Cuba became a Spanish colony. Exposed to diseases previously unknown in Cuba, many natives died while others were enslaved by the Spanish and later annihilated. Though some Cubans claim native ancestry, little of their culture and traditions survive. How sad. At least in the United States, Native Americans managed to survive the slaughter, deprivations, and other mistreatments by invading Europeans.

I was surprised to learn the University of Havana was founded in 1728. That's 130 years before Minnesota became a state. What a doofus I was. Seeing the splendor of the stately neoclassical buildings at the University of Havana constructed during the early 1900s, I realized that higher education has been highly valued in Cuba for centuries. Nilda told us 70 percent of the two thousand faculty members have master's degrees or doctorates. She noted about 65 percent of the seventeen thousand students at the University of Havana are women, and she added, "Cuban women would say it's because we are smarter." The remark drew laughs, at least from the women on our tour.

CHAPTER 2

A Heartbreaking Magnificence

In Havana, the country's history shows up in its stunning architecture. On our second day in Cuba, we passed block after block of large, majestic buildings. These massive structures range in style from Spanish baroque to French classicism to European art nouveau. But seeing the magnificent buildings became painful after a while. Many of these large apartment buildings in various sections of Havana are cracked, crumbling, and covered with mildew. Here and there, a random section of a building was under repair, but those sections were few and far between. We did not see the insides of these dilapidated buildings or even get close enough to touch them. But it's obvious that massive repairs are needed that will cost hundreds of millions of dollars and take decades. By contrast, we also saw homes, embassies, and diplomatic residences in the area called Miramar that are elegant, well maintained, and strikingly beautiful.

The contrast left me confused and saddened. I thought socialism advocates for a classless society in which the government controls all means of production and distribution of goods and no one owns private property. The idea is that if everyone works, everyone will reap the same benefits and prosper on a more equal basis. Clearly, that wasn't the case. Inequality still seemed widespread among the Cuban people.

Then I wondered, *Is Havana's neglected housing—which is subsidized by the Cuban government—any worse than the hundreds of blighted neighborhoods in Detroit, Chicago, Los Angeles, Phoenix, or Philadelphia? Or the rundown housing I've seen in rural America? Are we any better off than Cubans?*

Also scattered around Havana are dozens of Soviet-built apartment buildings—concrete, boxy structures with little or no architectural appeal. In short, they are ugly. Many of them, which seem especially graceless among the magnificent colonial buildings, also need extensive repairs.

This beautiful home in the Miramar area of Havana is one of many that stands in stark contrast to many other buildings in serious disrepair—cracked exterior walls, mildew, and crumbling facades that house less fortunate Havana residents.

What brought the housing to this terrible state? I know that when Fidel Castro took power, the new regime ended private ownership of housing. Renters were given control of their apartments, according to a 2014 Brookings Institution report on housing in Cuba. They paid half of their previous rent payment to the state. After five to ten years, they became full owners. Homeowners and landlords were compensated with a one-time lump sum or monthly payments for life. But many do not have money to maintain them.

At the same time, Cubans created their own real estate market, Cuban style. Under the law, they could swap residential housing units of equal value. "In the eyes of the law, homes were simply exchanged and no cash changed hands, even in a swap between a two-bedroom apartment and a four-bedroom house," according to the Brookings report. "In reality, side payments were routinely and discreetly made to compensate the person giving up the higher-value property."

Today, about 600,000 more housing units are needed in Cuba to adequately meet the citizens' needs, according to the latest Cuban government estimates. In 2012, Hurricane Sandy exacerbated the situation by destroying 22,396 homes in eastern Cuba.

The resulting housing shortage often means three or four generations live in one household. The typical configuration is for the grandparents to have the bedroom, parents sleep in the dining room, and children in the living room. Younger generations no longer want to live in such close quarters, giving rise to restlessness among young people, an increased divorce rate, and a declining birth rate as couples put off having children, Nilda told us.

Divorce, Cuban Style

Nilda's remark about divorce piqued my interest. She said divorce carries no social stigma and is quite common. The standard joke is that anyone whose parents stay together needs therapy. Various sources estimated that half to three-fourths of all marriages end in divorce. Divorce is inexpensive, costing about fifty Cuban pesos, or two dollars, she said. In uncontested cases, the couple splits everything fifty-fifty, and it's about as easy as getting a marriage certificate.

As the ever-inquisitive journalist, I sidled up to Nilda early in our trip to ask her for more specifics. The housing shortage makes it difficult for divorced couples to split up. Consequently, some divorced couples continue to live together because neither ex-spouse can find housing. I've known of a few divorced couples in the United States who lived under the same roof, but my guess is that it happens more often in Cuba.

Cubans who want to change their residence find that it is no easy matter. When Nilda decided to move to Havana from her hometown in the countryside and live with her uncle, she had to obtain permission from the authorities, she said. Before she could get the approval, an inspector visited her uncle's house to make sure there was adequate space for another occupant.

But housing reform is underway. In 2011, the Cuban government legalized free market sales of housing, among other measures. This new legal right to purchase a house has prompted Cubans to dream. Driving through one lovely Havana neighborhood in Miramar on our trip, Nilda playfully pointed to a majestic, gleaming white, two-story house as the one she planned to buy one day. She estimated it would cost about $200,000. I'm thinking that would be like me dreaming of purchasing a million-dollar home someday. I don't put my chances as any better than Nilda's.

Nevertheless, the Brookings Institution report called the legalization of residential real estate sales one of the most significant actions taken in Cuba's economic reform program. The reform counts as a human rights improvement because it expands economic freedom and advances private property rights, the report said.

Yet others worry that homelessness and inequality will grow with a private housing market, particularly for Afro-Cubans who were less likely to own property in prerevolutionary Cuba. "In Cuba, housing is seen as a right and not a commodity," wrote Jill Hamberg, a New York-based urban planning consultant who has written extensively on Cuba's housing issues. "Experience has shown the difficulty of eliminating the real estate market but leaving it completely free won't work either. The challenge will be to establish an enforceable legal framework that regulates the market to prevent speculation and artificial price hikes."

Neighbor or Spy?

Given the housing reforms, it will be fascinating to see what happens to the infamous block committees known as CDRs (Committees for the Defense of the Revolution). Every block has one. They have been controversial from their start in 1960.

Wary of a US invasion, the government formed CDRs to strengthen government policies and notify authorities of internal threats. The fear was embodied in the motto: "In a fortress under siege, all dissent is treason." A cynical view is that local CDR officials were there to spy on their neighbors and report troublemakers. Eventually, CDRs began addressing such issues as garbage collection, public health, and other civic concerns.

Such current-day scrutiny does not sit well with many Cubans. One woman told us about a local CDR official who grew suspicious that a neighbor had illicit income just because he had a garbage can full of empty soda cans. In reality, the neighbor was fond of soda and scrimped on other things so he could buy soft drinks.

As an American, I can't imagine living under such scrutiny of my personal habits. In my wonderful Saint Paul neighborhood, we have a block captain, but she does nothing more than arrange monthly neighborhood potlucks and keep us posted on events in our area. Am I too idealistic to think that such abuse doesn't happen in the United States? Or is it because my privileged, white, middle-class background never put me in situations where law enforcement or other officials questioned me unjustly?

We heard from several Cubans that CDRs appear to be losing influence, particularly among younger generations who tend to view them as a club for old folks. "Today, nobody wants to be president of their local CDR," one Cuban said. "There's no money in it. Just complaints."

Writing in a September 26, 2014, *Havana Times* article, Rogelio Manuel Diaz Moreno, who describes himself as an independent journalist, said: "People's exhaustion and the endless economic difficulties faced by the majority have undermined the government's rallying power, let alone that of the CDRs ... No less important is the fact that the country's economic difficulties have forced the majority of Cubans, CDR chairs included, to eventually become involved in illegal activities.

"To be able to get by, nearly everyone has learned to turn a blind eye on such activities," Moreno wrote. "Today, the CDR chair that is well-liked around the neighborhood is the one that does not meddle in the lives of neighbors and goes through the needed motions with higher-ups in order to show them what they want to see, without getting people in the neighborhood into trouble."

He went on to say that if anything can deal the CDRs their coup de grace, it is the legalization of private property and the accompanying rise of social classes. "[A]fter many years in which we believed we were blessed with equality, even the papers are beginning to defend the benefits of having some be more equal than others," he wrote. Some Cubans we met reinforced Moreno's view, including one who said, "It's not possible to keep everyone at the same level."

A Ray of Housing Hope

Once our tour bus rolled past the depressing and more densely populated areas of Havana, we arrived at the Muraleando Community Project. My mood lifted immediately. Energy and hope were in the air there. Suddenly, everyone in my tour group seemed invigorated.

Begun in 2001 to combat crime, this project is near an area that was once a garbage dump. In rebuilding the neighborhood, residents removed twenty tons of garbage and chased out four-pound rats with hairy tails. They built a school that started with thirteen children and had grown to two hundred students by 2014. The neighborhood is covered with colorful murals depicting Cuban life and sculptures made from old hubcaps, old telephones, and other detritus. They also produced freestanding paintings, sculptures, and Cuban dolls. The founders and some artists told us how they started offering art workshops. A strikingly good-looking young man, slender with muscled arms and dark skin set off by a white T-shirt, described through Nilda's translation how he left behind a life of petty thievery and took up the arts.

In 2001, local artists and residents created the Muraleando Community Project in a Havana barrio to combat crime. They began offering art workshops and spawned colorful murals in the neighborhood. A local resident told us of his rehabilitation from a life of crime, and a musical group with a songbird for a singer performed for us. Note the unusual homemade percussion instrument.

As some musicians began performing Cuban music with a joyful, irrepressible beat, many of my tour companions began dancing. Wildly! It was so much fun. I took pictures from all angles. Just listening to the woman vocalist, with the voice of a songbird, was pure heaven. Needless to say, I bought the group's CD called *Son Arte* and play it often. I never fail to sway to the music. This is one Cuban delight that I will never forget and can still experience.

CHAPTER 3

Preserving Old Havana

An open plaza in the Old Havana area has beautifully restored buildings.

Restaurants and other amenities are situated for easy access by tourists in Old Havana. This is just off one of the plazas.

A relief on the side of a building in Old Havana.

Restoration work is underway near the Plaza de Armas, one of four plazas in Old Havana.

Early in our trip, we took a walking tour of Old Havana, the original city. Now teeming with two million inhabitants, Havana was founded by the Spanish in 1519. Yikes, that was almost a hundred years before the first Europeans set foot in Minnesota. In the oldest part, narrow cobblestone streets wind around a mix of baroque and neoclassical monuments. Most of the buildings—private housing and shops with arcades, internal courtyards, and gates—abut one another. The area has been named a World Heritage Site by the United Nations Educational Scientific and Cultural Organization, also known as Unesco, calling it the most impressive historical city center in the Caribbean and one of the most notable in the American continent because of its architectural, historical, and environmental continuity. That claim certainly seems justified to me.

The area is a dream for any student of architecture, and even someone like me who simply appreciates beautiful buildings. I was awestruck by the extensive network of fortresses and walls created to protect the city from invaders. Built between the sixteenth and nineteenth centuries, these fortifications are some of the oldest and largest such structures standing in the Americas. One of the striking things about Old Havana is the four plazas—Plaza de Armas, Plaza de la Catedral, Plaza San Francisco de Asis, and Plaza Vieja—that frame the area. The Plaza de Armas marks the entrance of Old Havana, which once was one of the main centers for shipbuilding.

Facing the sea is a large fortress, one of a series of such structures built over the centuries. Walking on a narrow street beside one imposing structure, I could easily see marine fossils embedded in its limestone walls. The structure towered over me, about two stories high. I ran my hands over the walls and felt the mottled surface with its tiny seashells. They were not sharp to the touch but rough. Designed to protect Havana Bay, the structure has a durability that belies its age. Stopping for a moment, I imagined that if I had been living here centuries ago, I would have felt secure from invaders.

On the opposite side of the harbor from Old Havana, we also visited Castel Morro, a fort constructed between 1589 and 1630 to protect the entrance to the Havana harbor from invaders. "Morro" is Spanish for rock, which stands as a navigational landmark for seafarers. One evening we traipsed from the bus in a large parking lot filled with other tourist buses to a cobblestone plaza that ran the length of the wall. The rough-hewn stone walls are three feet thick. The fort itself is several stories high. No wonder it took more than forty years to build. Several hundred tourists were there to watch the guards march up to a cannon, accompanied by a drumbeat, and fire it at nine at night. Several large booms cracked the air. And that was pretty much it. The evening air was mild, and some drinks made it pleasant enough. But beyond that, there wasn't much there. Apparently, this nightly ritual started centuries ago to let Havana citizens know that it was time to take refuge behind the walls. For us, it was time to head back to the hotel and hit the sack. I was ready.

A mural in sepia tones in Old Havana.

The influence of the Roman Catholic Church is still visible in many places around Cuba. On our Old Havana tour, we walked to the middle of a plaza to see the Catedral de San Cristobal de la Habana, another exquisite architectural treasure. Jesuits began constructing the church in 1748 and finished in 1787—just eleven years after the American Revolution. Christopher Columbus's remains were interred there until 1898 when they were moved to Spain. Renovated in the early nineteenth century, the insides are somber, dominated by dark, heavy wood.

Growing up Catholic, I have been in many Catholic churches, cathedrals, and basilicas over the decades. Most of them are stunning in their décor. This church was plain, dark, and dreary, though I must admit it did seem like a solemn and sacred space. But it also gave me a spooky feeling. I didn't stay in it long, preferring to head outside into the sunshine. As I waited for my tour companions, I bought a long, cylindrical paper cone filled with salty peanuts to munch on for about ten cents.

Despite the age of most of the buildings in Old Havana, they are well preserved. To restore Old Havana, a private for-profit organization called Habaguanex operates restaurants, museums, gift shops, and hotels. Though independent, Habaguanex must give 45 percent of its profits to the government, our guide said. If I were Cuban, I might appreciate keeping the area attractive for tourists, but I also might resent the resources spent on restoring this area when housing in so many other parts of the city desperately needs renovation. On reflection, I thought about the controversial tax subsidies bestowed on the construction of professional sports stadiums that benefit rich team owners in cities around the United States. *Hmm. Another parallel to life in the United States,* I thought.

You can't visit Old Havana without noticing stray dogs everywhere. On this bright, sunny day, the nondescript mixed-breed mutts added a certain charm. But I'm a dog lover and was accustomed to seeing stray dogs wander the beaches and streets in Mexico and Costa Rica. The difference is these dogs wore tags with their names and photos provided by an animal protection organization. Often, they were curled up asleep in a corner of a street by a building or ambling down the streets, probably on a regular route of visiting shop owners likely to feed them. They paid scant attention to tourists.

Stray dogs are everywhere in Havana. Many have tags, which signify they are being taken care of by animal rights groups.

As we continued walking, we came to the Palacio de los Capitanes Genereales, a square building completed in 1792 in what's known as Cuban baroque style. This once was the official residence of the governors and now houses a museum. A square building, it has an arcade of arches supported by columns that provide a shaded walkway from the hot Caribbean sun.

The street into the courtyard is paved with wooden bricks, which are said to deaden the sound of horses' hooves. Who knew that noise pollution existed before the automobile? Almost instantly, I envisioned some governor's wife back in the 1800s demanding that her husband do something about noisy horse hooves that woke up her sleeping infant. By the way, you can hardly tell the bricks are wooden unless you look closely.

Overall, Old Havana has the feel of a small village somewhere in France or Spain. Americans and other foreigners were all over the place, making it one of the most tourist-infested places I visited in Cuba. The opportunity was not lost on the Cuban people. A man had a dog decked out in a tiny blue hat and coat sitting in a small box on the back of a bicycle. He was selling chocolates and small Cuban flags.

Down the street, an older woman clad in a white skirt and blouse with a blue headscarf topped with red cloth flowers sat in a chair puffing on a large Cuban cigar. I wondered whether she was there wanting people to take her picture and pay her. I took her picture from enough of a distance to avoid asking her permission. I didn't think more about her until I met a Cuban journalist in October 2016 covering the US presidential election. In a talk at a conference of women journalists, she showed a similar picture of a woman smoking a cigar. Explaining this image is a stereotype of Cuba that she detests, she said she wants Americans to view Cuba as a modern country. She also told us that Cubans were quite perplexed by the rise of Donald Trump and that she was struggling to explain his election to the Cuban people given his misogynistic treatment of women. We couldn't help her on that score. We didn't understand, either.

As we headed to a more modern section of Havana, Nilda took pains to point out when we were going through a seven-hundred-meter-long tunnel under Havana Bay. It took just a few minutes but symbolized a great distance to her. In a matter-of-fact tone, she noted that Batista had built the tunnel, which connected Old Havana with the eastern shore of the bay, in order to develop a modern suburb with large avenues, palm trees, and luxury buildings for the wealthy. The tunnel saved traveling twenty-five kilometers around the bay. Completed in 1958, the tunnel could be used only by the wealthy, she noted. Once Castro seized power, he opened the tunnel to all Cubans, who then had access to some of Havana's best beaches. Now, that's a plus for Fidel in my book.

Can a Cemetery Be Extraordinary?

Colon Cemetery offers stunning Italian marble headstones.

Visiting a cemetery ordinarily wouldn't be high on my sightseeing list. But the Colon Cemetery, or Cementerio de Cristóbal Colón, in the Vadado section of Havana is remarkable for its stunning Italian marble headstones. Established in 1876, the cemetery was originally intended for nobles, many of whom commissioned top architects to design and construct mausoleums, chapels, and family vaults reflecting their upper-class status. Now remains of revolutionary heroes, sports figures, and people from various walks of life are buried there too.

Known for its elaborately sculpted memorials with more than five hundred major mausoleums, chapels, and family vaults, the cemetery sprawls over 140 acres and still is in use today, though space is at a premium. In fact, the Central Chapel was hosting a funeral when we were there. Mourners in black filed into the small chapel.

The sky that day was a brilliant blue and contrasted sharply with what seemed like a sea of stark white, marble gravestones and monuments. I felt strangely uplifted and an immense sense of gratitude to be able to see these beautiful structures. And the cemetery guide named Irma, who could make a living as a stand-up comic, was a delight. As we trailed after her, she regaled us with intriguing stories involving some of the cemetery's rich and powerful occupants and their illicit love affairs, including one noblewoman whose lover escaped through her window. For some odd reason, one of my traveling companions asked her if Fidel Castro was sick. With a twinkle in her eye and a sly smile, she replied, "You know, I can't say," as though she was hiding a secret.

CHAPTER 4

The Dollar Rules

By this time in the tour, the details of Cuba's past became important. I learned that wars broke out three times in the 1800s between Cuban revolutionaries and the Spanish, who controlled the island. But mostly, I wanted to know when Americans' interest began in Cuba and why.

The answer should have been obvious. Americans saw Cuba as a place to make money. Sounds like American capitalism, doesn't it? In 1878, Americans began investing in Cuba's sugar and tobacco plantations. As decades passed, Cuban revolutionaries continued fighting. In 1895, the revolutionary, José Marti, launched an attack on the Spanish, but his forces were quickly thwarted. Later, he died in battle, becoming a hero to the Cuban people. Meanwhile, anti-Spanish fervor grew in the United States, largely fueled by Joseph Pulitzer's and William Randolph Hearst's New York newspapers, which printed exaggerated stories of Spanish atrocities against Cuban civilians. A few US officials floated the idea of annexing Cuba to protect America's economic interests, but nothing came of it.

As Nilda related Cuba's history, tidbits from my high school history class came back to me. Riots broke out in Havana in January 1898. The US consul-general cabled home fearing for the safety of Americans there. In response, the American battleship the USS *Maine* was sent to the Havana harbor.

A month later, the USS *Maine* blew up in the harbor, killing 258 crew members and sinking the ship. American newspapers blamed the Spanish. (Later investigations pointed to an internal explosion.) Soon, the cry, "Remember the *Maine*. To hell with Spain," led Congress to declare war in April 1898 with an amendment that the United States "leave the government and control of the island to its people," according to the Library of Congress website.

Ultimately, American forces arrived in Cuba. US troops, including Teddy Roosevelt's Rough Riders, went on to defeat the greatly outnumbered Spanish forces at San Juan Hill and Kettle Hill near Santiago de Cuba on July 1, 1898, according to the *New York Times* account. Eventually, the Spanish surrendered and ceded Cuba to the United States.

The United States established a provisional military government that ruled until 1902 and occupied Cuba two more times—from 1906 to 1909 and from 1917 to 1922. To this day, the Cuba government maintains that the United States illegally occupies Guantanamo Bay and refuses to cash the yearly $4,085 rent check that the United States pays to Cuba, according to a 2007 Reuters account.

Enviable Education?

As I learned about our shared history, the current interplay between the United States and Cuba started to make much more sense. But my curiosity soon turned to present-day life in Cuba. As we walked into yet another square in Old Havana, we saw a gaggle of schoolchildren sitting on the steps of a building, taking in an architecture lesson. I was bowled over. *First of all*, I thought, *Old Havana is a remarkable classroom.* The children could see their history literally in three dimensions and full color. What a way to instill a love of country, very much like US schoolchildren visiting our nation's capital. I never went to Washington, DC, as a child, but my family visited Springfield, Illinois, when I was about eight. We toured Abraham Lincoln's house and a nearby monument. I treasure that experience to this day.

The Cuban schoolchildren melted my heart immediately. Dressed in bright white blouses and shirts with red ties and navy shorts or skirts, they had a beautiful range of skin tones from olive to dark brown. I was enchanted, partly because they behaved like any group of American children. Some were paying attention. Others seemed distracted.

Regardless, they represent Cuba's remarkable education system. And that's not just my opinion. The World Bank cited Cuba for its high-quality education system in 2014 in a study of education systems in Caribbean countries. "Indeed, only Cuba, where education has been the top priority since 1959, has a truly efficient education system and high-quality teachers," the report said. "In terms of education, this Caribbean country has no cause to be envious of even the most developed nations. The Caribbean island is also the nation in the world that allocates the highest share of its national budget, 13 percent, to education."

But it wasn't always that way. In 1953 before Castro took over, only 76 percent of the population was literate. "Neither health care nor education reached those rural Cubans at the bottom of society," a BBC documentary noted. "Illiteracy was widespread, and those lucky enough to attend school seldom made it past the first or second grades." Under Castro, attendance became compulsory for children from ages six to sixteen. That policy paid off. Within a few decades, literacy reached 99.8 percent. Nilda offered firsthand evidence. "My grandmother learned to read and write because of the revolution," she said.

At the same time, there's no doubt that Fidel Castro used the schools to indoctrinate younger generations in socialism and Communism. I have an American friend who offers a different view. Married to a Cuban American, she is a Spanish teacher who has visited Cuba several times. Her take is that the education system is not all it's cracked up to be and that literacy is not as high as reported.

Nevertheless, education is free, beginning with daycare and continuing through college. Students attend primary school for six years, then a basic secondary or high school for three to four years. Once they complete the basic secondary level, they can enter preuniversity education and technical or professional training. They take placement tests to gain entrance to a university or trade school. Students can earn a master's degree or a doctorate in sciences at one of sixty-eight universities, colleges, and other centers. And they leave with no student loan debt! Is this a system based only on merit, not on who can afford to pay? I hate to think about how much it will cost for my six grandchildren to earn college degrees. Perhaps the United States could learn something from Cuba.

For me, the impressive part about the educational system is that the Cuban government offers specialized schools at the elementary, intermediate, and advanced stages for students interested in music, painting, sculpture, dance, ballet, and other performing arts. The same goes for young people who excel in sports and have the skills to pursue careers in these fields by attending schools at the midlevel and higher. There's no doubt that American sports teams have benefited from Cuba's training of athletes. Since 1963, dozens of Cuban baseball and soccer players have defected from Cuba to play ball. A few have become big stars winning multimillion-dollar contracts.

Schoolchildren are being taught about architecture in Old Havana. Cuba has a highly regarded education system, especially compared to other Caribbean countries.

As Elio Delgado, writing in the *Havana Times,* put it, "This instruction ensures that no talent in any of these art forms goes ignored or disregarded." We saw this firsthand during a visit to a community project for young adults with Down syndrome in the town of Pinar del Rio, a place that dates back to 1778, by the way. My cynical side emerged at this point. *Why were they showing us this? Was this the government's attempt to counter critics' charges about the inadequacy of services for disabled children?*

Education in Cuba for children with mental and physical disabilities is free. Many are cared for in their homes and hospitals by itinerant teachers. Parents are paid to stay home with their children, Nilda told us. Some

Cubans have complained that special education schools serve only about 22 percent of the disabled population.

But it is pretty darned hard to remain skeptical when you're watching some darling children and enthusiastic adults coaching them. Founded by a local painter, Jesus Carrete, the project is known as Proyecto Comunitario con Amore & Esperanza, which roughly translated means Community Project for Love and Hope. Aimed at encouraging the youth to attain personal fulfillment, develop artistic self-expression, and build social integration skills, the project has humble surroundings—a few small rooms and an outdoor courtyard in the back.

Besides watching the young people produce some impressive artwork, we were treated to a show that included singing and dancing. Clad in colorful costumes of bright yellow and red, the girls twirled around on the makeshift stage. The boys, dressed in white pants and loose-fitting shirts, danced, too. One boy moved deliberately and slowly to the music. I was taken aback by their intense concentration while they performed. *This is a big deal for them,* I thought. My throat tightened. My eyes watered. I felt deeply moved by this artistic expression. I was not alone. Everyone in my group seemed to appreciate it. We applauded loudly when they were done.

I later discovered a report by the Center for Human Rights and Humanitarian Law on its website in March 2014 that said many Cubans with disabilities lack essential services, though it acknowledged that Cuba provides about 150 pesos per month to such persons. In a hearing before the Inter-American Commission on Human Rights, some unnamed petitioners called on the Cuban government to promote a comprehensive education program for children with disabilities, according to the center's website. About 367,000 people or 3 percent of Cuba's population have disabilities, the center said. Cuba had no representative at the hearing.

In the town of Pinar del Rio, a community project for young adults with Down syndrome encourages the youths' development, particularly through artistic expression and social integration.

CHAPTER 5

Curiosities, Frustrations, and Delights

One of the most curious surprises for me was the attitude that Cubans displayed about the Soviet Union. More than once, I got the sense that Cubans have not embraced Soviet and Russian culture. Aside from the ugly Soviet-era buildings and cars, I couldn't spot any lasting cultural influences. Cubans speak in a matter-of-fact tone about the role that the Soviets played in their economy, but I couldn't detect any warmth or fondness there. Our guide noted her mother has a Soviet-made washing machine that still works decades after it was made.

To me, this dearth of Soviet influence seemed strange given that Cuba became almost totally dependent on the Soviet Union beginning in 1960. The Soviets bought up Cuba's sugar crop when no one else would and sold oil to Cuba at below-market rates. In exchange, Cuba adopted some political reforms requested by the Soviets and stood as a partner against the United States. Those subsidies and other benefits lasted until the Soviet Union collapsed in 1991.

My hunch was confirmed when I returned and found a 1978 article in the *Wilson Quarterly*. The author, Richard Fagen, wrote then that he was walking with a Cuban friend in a once fashionable section of Havana when he spotted a pair of massive high-rise buildings facing the ocean. His friend told him the buildings were living quarters for Soviet and East European technicians and their families. When Fagen asked his Cuban friend what influence the Soviets had on Cuba, his friend replied: "It doesn't exist. We simply owe them our lives." Noting the profound influence that America has had on Cuba and Latin America, Fagen went on to say that the "tracelessness" of Soviet influence on Cuba is astonishing. And the more I think about it, the more I agree.

Amid all this history and culture, I spotted some decidedly peculiar Cuban practices—at least from an American perspective. If you want to hail a taxi, you must know the right sign to stop the right one. For example, if you're on Third Avenue headed to Miramar, you must raise three fingers. Otherwise, no taxi will stop. Few foreigners bother with buses, preferring the *máquinas*, which use large, old, American-made cars as taxis. They run specific routes and typically charge ten Cuban pesos for a ride. Taxi drivers and others who work in the private sector pay a fixed tax each month based on the government's estimate of how much they make. Anyone caught evading taxes faces a huge fine of eighty thousand Cuban pesos.

Another oddity is the money. Two currencies exist side by side— Cuban pesos and convertible pesos (abbreviated as CUCs and pronounced *kooks*). One CUC is worth about one US dollar or twenty-five Cuban pesos. Convertible pesos are needed because Cuban pesos are not worth anything on the international market. Most Cubans use Cuban pesos, while most tourists use CUCs.

The tricky part is both currencies look similar, so tourists need to understand the markings to distinguish between them. All convertible pesos have the phrase "convertible pesos" on the front and back. Peso notes depict historical events, slogans, and cultural, educational, or agricultural achievements, while the CUCs have pictures of monuments. Awhile ago, the government announced plans to end this confusing situation. But it's not clear yet when that will happen.

During my trip, American credit cards were not accepted. Right after President Obama began trying to open up relations with Cuba, MasterCard announced that it would start accepting credit card purchases in Cuba in 2015. By January 2018, that hadn't happened. The result is inconvenience for Americans who visit Cuba and spend less and reduced profits for Cubans. I find this situation exasperating as stubborn politicians in both countries cling to outmoded ideas. Enough already! In spite of this situation, tourism became the country's top industry in the 1990s, surpassing the sugar trade, which traditionally ranked at the top.

Cuba has one other frustration for visitors in common with other Central American countries I have visited. Many of the cobblestone streets and paths are in disrepair or have badly worn patches. Often, curbs and steps are uneven. This means you must watch your step. My friend fell on some wet stones that had turned slippery, but he wasn't hurt. Bifocal wearers should be particularly cautious.

One delight that makes Cuba enjoyable is the absence of distracting TV screens in restaurants, bars, and on the street. Given the ubiquitous screens in every American bar and restaurant, and at every airport gate, I found this to be an immense relief. In fact, I loved being blissfully ignorant of what else was going on in the world when I was in Cuba. Even as a newshound, I was far too absorbed in what I was experiencing to miss my daily news fix. The result was a lot more conversation with my companions. We talked a lot about our lives back home. My companions were, for the most part, well traveled and highly educated. One was an emergency room physician. Another was a heart surgeon. Another was a retired US attorney. Others were educators and higher education administrators or engaged in a variety of other professions.

Many socialist practices continue in Cuba. For example, every young person owes the government three years of service after high school or university. Frankly, this makes a lot of sense of me. I wish America had a national service requirement. Though we have AmeriCorps Vista, a national service program for young people designed to alleviate poverty, it is voluntary. And I believe it's on Trump's chopping block. In Cuba, an individual's skills and talents are supposed to be matched to a social service job. For example, Nilda, who is fluent in French and English, served as a translator before she became a tour guide. Young men who finish high school and don't go further in the educational system serve all three years in the military. Male university students serve one of their three years in the military.

Laughing Matters

Early in our trip, I began to get a sense of the Cuban character. For one thing, they have a puckish sense of humor. Perhaps it's not surprising. After enduring fifty years of hardships, they must have found that humor and an irreverent attitude about themselves, their government, and life in general are essential to surviving and being resilient. Whatever the cause, these qualities now seem built into their character.

Conner Gorry, a journalist and blogger, confirmed my view. In his blog, *Here is Havana*, he wrote: "These folks love to share stories, jokes, and the occasional tall tale, and use their verbal prowess to enliven, laugh, and woo; it is what has enabled these people to resist so much for so long. Even without Spanish skills or a translator, if you're not laughing a lot on a visit here, you're doing something wrong in my personal and professional opinion."

And in the book *Laughing Under Castro: A 50-year revolution? You must be kidding!*, author Modesto Arocha compiled jokes told behind closed doors among trusted friends, noted Laura Turner Garrison on Splitsider, a website about comedy and the people who create it. An example: *As the small jet lands at Havana's Jose Marti airport, the pilot announces, "Welcome to Cuba. Please set your watches back fifty years."*

"Taken all at once, the situation in Cuba seems not at all funny, but horrifying," Garrison wrote. "But, laughter is a universal coping mechanism and just what the well-trained Cuban doctor ordered."

Nilda, our guide, certainly had her laugh lines down, though none of them made fun of the government. Once she quipped: "When you have one Cuban, you have five different opinions." She also let us in on some slang. "Mango," for example, is a synonym for "sexy." Cubans love mangoes, she explained. The women in my group picked up on this term immediately.

Soon after she introduced us to that expression, we were returning to our hotel from dinner at a restaurant when Nilda suddenly announced that the bus driver would make a quick stop. Since we were so close to her home, we would drop her off, she explained. She also promised to introduce us to her husband. Once the bus stopped, a slender, dark-haired guy with a chiseled face and a ready smile appeared out of the darkness. Without hesitation, the American women on the bus yelled out, "Mango, mango." Her husband blushed and seemed embarrassed. Nilda just laughed. The evening's events left me satiated by the food, amused by my companions, and savoring the experience.

CHAPTER 6

The Hard Life

Yes, my traveling companions and I laughed a lot during our trip. Cubans are very good at entertaining. Sometimes, however, I would catch myself feeling uncomfortable that I was enjoying myself so much. I wondered about the hardships imposed on the Cuban people by their government and mine that we weren't seeing. Still, we got a few glimpses. On one of our longer road trips to the countryside, Nilda told us a particularly poignant story.

She recalled when she was a seven-year-old growing up in rural Cuba. She remembers being enchanted when her mother told her the flower petals floating in her bath water would entice the fairies to kiss her as she was sleeping. She lived with this illusion until she realized years later that her mother had used the fantasy to disguise the fact that her middle-class family had no bath soap. It was 1993. Two years earlier, the Soviet Union had collapsed, leaving Cuba with no country willing to purchase its sugar crop. Factories shut down. Jobs ended. Cuba's economy nearly ground to a halt, already hamstrung by heavy-handed government control and weakened by the US trade embargo then thirty years old. Officially, these years came to be known as the "Special Period."

It wasn't until 2000 that life improved. Hugo Chávez, then the president of Venezuela, began subsidizing oil. The annual aid that Chávez provided—in petroleum, investments, and currency—came to surpass that of the Soviet Union, and by 2010 would total nearly $13 billion, 21

34

percent of Cuba's GDP that year, wrote Enrique Krauze in the *New York Review of Book*.

As a result, Chávez was a much-loved figure in Cuba. One road sign we saw about 170 km outside of Havana read, "Chávez—our great friend." During our trip, Cubans were nervous about what would happen since Chavez had died a year earlier.

In December 2014, the *Miami Herald* reported that Venezuela ships one hundred thousand barrels a day of subsidized oil to Cuba. In return, Venezuela receives thousands of doctors, teachers, and some military advisers from Cuba. "But with falling oil prices eating into Venezuelan revenue, high inflation, food shortages and a newly minted law from Washington sanctioning Venezuelan officials who engaged in human rights abuses, things are not going well for Cuba's ideological soul mate," the *Herald* noted. "It's not so much a question of Venezuela not wanting to help Cuba but more of how long it will have the capacity to continue." Since then, Venezuela economy has gone down the drain, and its democracy is in a death spiral. Without Venezuela's economic support, the obvious question becomes, could this loss of economic trade with Venezuela underlie Cuba's motivation for reestablishing diplomatic ties with the United States?

An Ad-Free Economy

But let's not dwell on dreary economics. In fact, it is hard to stay serious for long in Cuba. The warm sun, the good cheer, and the rum are just too enticing to resist. On one sunny morning, my group headed out from Havana to Cuba's lowland plains. We traveled on a smooth four-lane highway. After a short while, the only thing in view was a natural landscape. Suddenly, it struck me: no intrusive billboards beckoned one to buy something. Cuba is free of advertising. Once in a while, a roadside sign espoused a political message, such as "Free the Cuban Five" (who have since been freed). But even those signs were sparse.

One of the infrequent road signs espousing Castro's philosophy that reads:
The Revolution is one beautiful and indestructible reality.

What a welcome respite, was my first thought. In the United States, ads promoting goods and services in our capitalistic economy saturate us nearly every waking moment. It's hard to go to a restroom in a US restaurant without seeing an ad on a toilet stall door. My second thought: *Advertising would be pointless here. Cubans don't have the money to buy consumer goods.* They could barely afford necessities. The average wage was about twenty-five dollars a month in 2015, according to Cuba's National Office of Statistics, though they have free medical care, access to a free education, including universities, and some routine expenses are modest. Bus rides cost about five cents. Movies are a dime. A 2016 survey by a marketing firm showed, however, that more than two-thirds of Cubans earned more than fifty dollars a month. While most Cubans get by, they have few legal means to prosper.

On that day, we were headed to Mantanzas, a city that dates back to 1693. That's a mere seventy years after the Pilgrims first landed at Plymouth Rock. Located about sixty-five miles from Havana, this city of about 150,000 has been called the "Athens of Cuba" and is said to have given birth to the rumba and the *danzón*, Cuba's national dance. Oddly enough, there was nothing touristy about it. But the lack of tourist spots added to its charm for me. It felt like the real Cuba as we glimpsed Cubans going about their lives. Residents whizzed by on motor scooters or walked briskly along the streets. We saw students sitting alongside a creek relaxing and reading.

The city is the capital of the province by the same name, which translates as "massacres." Ravaged by pirates in the 1600s, this province extends the entire width of the island. On the southern shore of the province is the infamous Bahia de Cochinos, known to Americans as the Bay of Pigs.

In 1961, armed Cuban exiles, funded by the US Central Intelligence Agency, landed in an attempt to overthrow the Castro government. Poor planning and inadequate equipment thwarted the invaders, who were soon caught. The short-lived invasion was a fiasco, not one of America's finer moments. As a consequence, Castro began to rely heavily on the Soviet Union for protection and economic subsidies. He also turned away from his democratic ideals, which he had espoused early on.

Now I started to wonder whether US government actions thwarted Cuba's chances of becoming a democracy. After all, many of the Cubans who fled when Castro seized power had grown wealthy under Batista. I know they left their homes and businesses behind and had to rebuild their lives in America. I'm glad we welcomed them and happy that many have prospered. But did they support fair wages and democratic elections for the Cuban people? I felt conflicted about the motivations of all the parties. Was anyone putting the welfare of poor Cubans ahead of making money? I can't say, even now, that I know the answer to that question. What's worse, I worry that President Trump may harm efforts to improve life for the Cuban people with his pigheaded ideas.

The Triolet Family Pharmacy in Mantanzas, which dates back to 1879, is in stellar condition. The whole place is a work of art with its dark polished wood, rows of white apothecary jars, and gadgets from the era. Mantanzas is about sixty-five miles from Havana and was established in 1693.

Fortunately, during my trip, I could focus on the charming bits of Cuba. One such notable spot in the city of Mantanzas was the Triolet Family Pharmacy, which is now a museum. A feast for the eyes, the pharmacy has large masses of polished dark wood cabinetry, ornate porcelain jars, and displays of many original pharmaceutical implements and supplies that show off the striking beauty of its well-preserved 1880s atmosphere. Rows and rows of instruments were neatly arranged on shelves. Drawers once filled with medicines lined the walls.

Founded in 1882 by a Dr. Ernesto Triolet, a French doctor and his brother-in-law, Dr. Juan Fermín de Figueroa, a Cuban physician, the pharmacy was in business until 1964. It's worth seeing, but this tourist attraction provided a stark indication that this city and its people had seen better days. After a short walk, we arrived at the Hotel Velasco, another neoclassic building with marble, tile floors, and dark wood. We had one of the best meals of our trip, featuring red snapper, rice, and artfully arranged cooked vegetables along with a delicious chocolate ice cream topped with a cherry sauce. The dark chocolate flavor delighted my taste buds as it blended in with the rich, creamy ice cream and the succulent, bright red sauce.

Here is just one pretty and tasty meal we had. We ate in many lovely restaurants and hotels as well as some that were more ordinary.

After lunch, we paid a short visit to the Ediciones Vigia Publishing Collective. It's quite a small-scale operation but impressive. Local craftsmen and women produce limited-edition handmade books of literary value that become works of art. Established in 1985, Ediciones Vigia encourages artists to use discarded materials, such as butcher paper, leaves, fabric, and other materials. They craft no more than two hundred copies of each book. This spot wasn't a showstopper for me, but as I watched the artists at work, I certainly appreciated their intensity, their clever designs, and the attention to detail that make their work so noteworthy.

On our way out of town, we stopped at a recently renovated former church known as Ermita de Monserrate. Situated on one of the highest points in the area with a sweeping panoramic view overlooking city of Matanzas and the Yumni Valley, the imposing white church is a lovely example of Spanish colonial architecture. A climb up the bell tower stairs is worth it for the view. You can even ring the bell. But the best part was a concert by a string group, Grupo Fantasia, consisting of a father and three daughters (two violins, a viola, and piano). They played an impressive array of classical music that included Mozart and Vivaldi and some Gershwin.

As music teachers, the father, Alberto, told us their students always start by learning classical music. Schools provide instruments to the children, by the way. Of course, I bought their CD. I still play it and remember the polished, dark-grained wood pews against the stark white walls and the sweet harmonies of warm notes reverberating through the church. I remember feeling so peaceful and calm.

Though I hadn't expected to hear classical music in Cuba, I loved it, especially since it was so well played. What I realize now is that this familiar music engendered a feeling of kinship with the Cuban people. In short, I felt at home and that they value the same things I do. Indeed, most of the musicians who performed for us played many familiar American pieces from Duke Ellington, Frank Sinatra, and Billy Joel, as much as they played Latin or Cuban music. Somehow, in my presumptuous, narrow-minded view of Cuba, I had thought they would have avoided American music.

Adding to my chagrin was learning from some musicians in the string group and several other groups that they had performed in the United States. *What?* I thought. *Hadn't the embargo and our longstanding frosty relationship prevented Cuban musicians from touring in the United States?* Apparently not.

However, there was a catch. On those US performance tours, they had not been allowed to receive money, one told us. I don't know if that rule was imposed by the Cuban government, the US government, or both.

Local craftsmen and women produce handmade books of literary value that become works of art at the Ediciones Vigia Publishing Collective in Matanzas, a city on the north shore of the island and about sixty miles east of Havana.

A Bit of Heaven

Little did we know that after the concert the best part of the day was still ahead. Venturing about two hours almost straight north, we arrived at Varadero, the largest seaside resort area in Cuba. What a spot. It has more than fifty hotels. We stayed at the Melia Las Americas, built by the Spanish. It is large, modern, and as beautiful as any I've seen in Mexico or Costa Rica. The Cuban government owns 51 percent while foreign entities own the other 49 percent. Hotel workers are paid by the government.

Varadero is also known as a "frozen zone," which means ordinary Cubans cannot move there unless they have relatives they can live with. Here, it's easy to escape any unpleasant thought about the plight of the Cuban people. The beach is sandy. The waves splash methodically on the shore. The sun reflects on the water like diamonds. Troubles for anyone seem far from this spot.

Near our hotel is the luxurious du Pont mansion, now known as Hotel Xanadu. Built as a retirement home in 1927 by the French American millionaire Irenee Dupont de Nemour, the house was confiscated in 1960 by the Cuban government and now operates as a tourist attraction with a bar and restaurant. The third floor offers a spectacular 360-degree view of the ocean, sandy beaches, and verdant land adjoining a well-manicured eighteen-hole golf course.

While sipping my mojito and taking in the view, I started thinking about how Americans are losing out. If it were easier to travel to Cuba, Americans would flock there. What if US companies could invest there and make some dough. *Why let the Spanish make all the money?* I wondered. *Even if they do have to share it with the Cuban government? The US embargo and travel ban is crazy.*

As the liquor took effect, we checked into a beautifully sunny room with a balcony overlooking the ocean at the Melia Las Americas. The room was so inviting that it almost took my breath away. The décor was a lovely shade of orange, not too bright but invigorating. Sheer curtains fluttered in the breeze. I felt totally relaxed. A few minutes later, I gave into the urge to take a nap. It was a delicious and dreamy sleep.

CHAPTER 7

The Rise of the Castros

Staying in this seaside paradise was short-lived. The next morning, we were in the hotel lobby by seven o'clock, eager to discover the culture of central Cuba. Specifically, we went to Santa Clara in the province of Villa Clara. During the 165-mile trip, Nilda gave us another Cuban history lesson. It was unsettling, to say the least, and offered some insights on Castro's rise.

And as I think back now in 2018 on that day in Cuba, it strikes me as sad that the United States supported a series of Cuban dictators from the 1920s to the 1940s. The Cuban leaders joined with plantation owners to enrich themselves and hold down the Cuban people. Calls for reform from university students and sugar workers went unheeded. Meanwhile, US tourists began flocking to Cuba in the Jazz Age, fueling a boom in American-owned hotels and restaurants.

At the same time, General Fulgencio Batista, who was chief of the armed forces, began accumulating political power by backing the dictators. In 1940, he was elected president on a populist platform. A constitution was adopted that embraced progressive ideas, including labor rights and health care, though it didn't seem to do much good. Once Batista's term ended in 1944, he went to Florida, only to return in 1952 to seek power again. Though an election was set to take place, Batista seized control, suspended the constitution, and revoked most political liberties, including the right to strike.

Here's where Fidel Castro comes into play. At odds with Batista from the start, Fidel Castro had become politically active in law school. The son of a prosperous sugar farmer, he intended to run for a seat in the Cuba House of Representatives in 1952, according to Jennifer Rosenberg, a twentieth-century history expert. After Batista canceled the election, Castro went to court to oust Batista. When that strategy failed, Castro organized a group of rebels and began plotting Batista's demise.

Now I was beginning to see the impact of this history on the people. When our tour bus turned onto a two-lane road, I gazed out the window to a scene that looked as though we were back in the 1900s. Horse-drawn carts clip-clopped on the road. Oxen pulled plows in the fields. Children were being bathed in a washtub on a flat-roofed building. Though these quaint images made for good tourist photos, they do not help Cuba advance in the twenty-first century. Instead, these images show a nation, at least in rural areas, mired in a distant past.

In rural parts of Cuba, travel by horse cart is not unusual.

On a Santa Clara rooftop, two children play while a woman washes clothes.

My feelings were confirmed once I returned and found out that before Castro seized power, profound inequalities existed, particularly between urban and rural areas and between whites and blacks. "In the countryside, some Cubans lived in abysmal poverty," according to a PBS documentary, "Pre-Castro Cuba." "Sugar production was seasonal, and the *macheteros*—sugarcane cutters who only worked four months out of the year—were an army of the unemployed, perpetually in debt and living on the margins of survival. Many poor peasants were seriously malnourished and hungry.

"Neither health care nor education reached those rural Cubans at the bottom of society," the documentary said. "Illiteracy was widespread, and those lucky enough to attend school seldom made it past the first or second grades." Now 99 percent of Cubans over the age of fifteen are literate, according to the Central Intelligence Agency's Book of Facts.

Batista aligned with owners of the largest sugar plantations and made lucrative deals with large US-based corporations and the American mafia, who controlled drug, gambling, and prostitution businesses in Havana. He quelled student demonstrations by tightening media censorship and waging a campaign of wide-scale violence, torture, and public executions, ultimately killing thousands.

How many generations of Cubans have been held down by ruthless dictators who held power merely to enrich themselves? The sobering note for me: until 1959, the Batista government received financial, military, and logistical support from the United States. Once again, we were on the wrong side of democracy. It makes my heart sink to begin counting how many Central and South American dictators we have supported. On the other hand, the Castro brothers, who haven't seemed interested in riches and fame, had promised to help Cuba's downtrodden people and create a democracy. Clearly, that promise has not been fulfilled and still fosters resentment, anger, and despair in Cuba and in the United States.

Given these conditions, is it any wonder that revolutionaries like Fidel and Raúl Castro arose? As Nilda recounted how the Castros started their insurgency in July 1953, I had to admire their chutzpah. With only 160 men, the Castro brothers attacked a well-armed and well-manned military base. This became known as the Twenty-Sixth of July Movement, which started the Cuban Revolution. Sixty of Castro's comrades died in that failed attempt. Both Castro brothers were captured and tried. On being found guilty, Castro declared, "Condemn me. It does not matter. History will absolve me." Though given a fifteen-year sentence, he was released two years later in May 1955.

The Castros fled to Mexico, where they met Ernesto Guevara, popularly known as Che. In November 1956, the Castros, Che, and a cadre of fighters crowded onto a small yacht named *Granma* and headed to Cuba. They made it but barely. The boat is remarkably small. In viewing it, I marveled at how a boat designed for twenty-five passengers could carry eighty men. Now enclosed in glass, the *Granma* stands in a Havana park that displays tanks and jeeps. The delivery truck used in the 1957 assault on the presidential palace and a turbine from the U-2 spy plane supposedly downed during the 1962 Cuban Missile Crisis also are on display.

But it wasn't until I walked around Santa Clara, a city of about 242,000, that the full force of Castro's revolution hit me. The dull gray sky was overcast. The bus stopped on a busy street. We filed off and walked a few yards to a wide plaza, the site of the Battle of Santa Clara. It was in this spot that Tren Blindado, Batista's armored train, was derailed by Castro's rebels with a bulldozer in December 1958. The famous bulldozer is mounted on a concrete base and angled as though it's about to charge into something. Two derailed train cars jut out awkwardly from the tracks. Now rusting red hulks, they still have mounted machine guns poking out their ports.

My traveling companions seemed a bit taken aback by this visual tour de force. Some climbed up on the rail cars and peered inside. Others looked as though they were analyzing how the bulldozer tore up the tracks and led to the derailment. They didn't say much. Everyone was snapping pictures. I shot a few photos myself. But mostly I stood transfixed by the thought that this site was the last conflict of the Cuban Revolution. After the Battle of Santa Clara, Batista fled Cuba. The Castros took over.

Tren Blindado, an armored train derailed with a bulldozer by Castro's compatriot, Ernesto Guevara, popularly known as Che, in December 1958 still stands on the memorial grounds in Santa Clara.

The bulldozer stands as a permanent symbol of resistance, a rebel turned icon.

A few miles from the derailed train is the Ernesto Guevara Sculptural Complex. Che led the guerilla troops who triumphed in Santa Clara. Later, he held various positions in Castro's government. In 1967, he died attempting to foment a revolution in Bolivia. Since then, Guevara has become a figure who symbolizes rebellion and socialism. He is less frequently remembered for ordering prisoners executed without trial in Cuba.

The memorial to him, set in a large open park, includes a twenty-two-foot-high bronze statue of Che, a museum, and the mausoleum that holds his remains and those of twenty-nine combatants who died with him. On this misty day, the place had a particularly somber quality to it. Call me jaded, but I wasn't impressed with the statue of Che outside, perhaps because it was one of the few times I was chilly in Cuba. I didn't hang around it long. The mausoleum, however, evoked a quiet peaceful dignity. My group moved through without speaking. It was dark and quiet inside. The walls are thin, dark gray slabs of rough-edged stones and dull-colored plaques naming each person. Nothing soft here. All of it symbolized Che's strength and power.

The adjoining museum offered a well-laid-out narrative of Che's life. Large pictures showed him smoking cigars and playing golf. His gun, binoculars, water bottle, medical certificates, and other mementoes were displayed in glass cases. And, of course, there were pictures with Fidel, or El Comandante. Seeing all this hit me hard and made me teary-eyed. I started thinking about my late husband, Jack, who admired Che. In fact, a large poster of Che still hangs in my basement, what I used to call his man cave. He had died five years earlier. Somehow, I can't bring myself to take the poster down.

I'm not sure why Jack was so enraptured with Che, other than the fact that Jack was always a bit of a rebel himself. He had so wanted to visit Cuba but refused to do it illegally. In 2008, he died of a sudden heart attack. I'm still sad whenever I think of him missing out on this trip. But he was not Che's only fan.

Cubans seem to idolize Che. His image—in various renditions— proliferates in street vendors' stalls all over Havana. I bought one. "Personally, I think he would die if he saw all the commerce with his pictures," Nilda said. On the other hand, pictures of the Castro brothers are almost nowhere to be found. Nilda explained such a display would conflict with the Castros' philosophy that its leaders should not be glorified.

When she said that, I had to laugh knowing that US presidents and governors *always* have their pictures posted anywhere, seeing it as politically advantageous. The White House website, for example, featured a large picture on its home page of President Obama and now shows a triumphant photo of President Trump. By contrast, the Cuban government website had thumbnail-size pictures of "Compañero Fidel" and President Raúl Castro.

After Fidel died on November 25, 2016, I wondered whether Fidel's pictures would become just as pervasive as Ché's. The "official" answer came after a week of national mourning. President Raúl Castro announced his government would prohibit the name of streets and monuments after his brother and bar construction of statues of him in keeping with Fidel's desire to avoid a cult of personality, according to an Associated Press story. I'm skeptical that this edict will hold. But at least the Castros pay lip service to humility, not like our presidents who probably begin planning their presidential libraries soon after they're elected.

I suspect, like me, most Cubans have mixed emotions about Fidel Castro. He clearly has held great sway over his people. As one Cuban put it: "Fidel, when he was speaking, could make you believe the sky was pink even though it was blue." In 2017, that sounds eerily prescient of Donald Trump.

Gray Is Good

Santa Clara held one other gem for me. We visited a senior center called Joy of Life. Housed in a few small nondescript rooms in a building on a narrow street, the center is one in a network of senior clubs around the country. Membership costs one Cuban peso a month. A senior citizen myself, I was eager to find out about life for older Cubans. After all, the Cuban population, like that in many developed countries, is aging. More than 16 percent are now over age sixty. And the number of children per family is shrinking. Nilda noted that her grandmother was one of nineteen children, her father was one of five children, and she is one of two children. By the way, birth control pills and abortions are free for young women, age sixteen and older.

In Santa Clara, we visited Joy of Life, a club for seniors. The club's president told us, "This is a very happy club." The elders told us that older people are well respected in Cuba.

At Joy of Life, we met with about a dozen retirees who greeted us warmly. They included a former professor, accountant, nurse, teacher, and a mechanic named Rafael, who told us he worked seventeen years past retirement age because he wanted to. He was eighty-two when we met him. Almost instantly, we felt a sense of comradery since most of the Americans on my tour were in their sixties and beyond. Their infectious smiles won my heart and admiration.

The club's president, Nenita, seventy-eight, a retired professor, told us, via Nilda's translation, "This is a very happy club. We celebrate everything. We do all sorts of things, such as camping, one-day excursions and sports events. The purpose is to improve the quality of life." Three times a year, they collect household items, toys, and clothing and give them to orphans. They told us that older people are well respected in Cuba and described old age as "youth accumulated." *Hmm,* I wondered, *would most older citizens in the United States say they are treated with respect?*

Founded thirty-one years ago, the club has about 120 members, ranging in age from their seventies to their nineties. That's not surprising given that life expectancy in Cuba has gone from sixty-nine in the 1960s to seventy-eight today, which is similar to that of the United States. Women can retire at age sixty; men at sixty-five. Some older Cubans work longer because they need the money or because they're still needed. Recently, Cuba began allowing retirees to return to work and still collect their pensions to alleviate a worker shortage.

As we munched on cookies and sipped drinks, our newfound friends treated us to a delightful display of the danzón, a national dance that seemed scandalous when it was introduced in 1879. Couples would dance together closely with sinuous hip movements. Invited to try it, a few of us gave this dance a whirl while a record played in the background. A Cuban gentleman took me in his arms. I place one hand on his shoulder, and he gently guided my steps in a square pattern. The dance was pretty easy even for a klutz like me. Most of my colleagues were content to sit and watch quietly.

What Slavery Hath Wrought

Heading out from Santa Clara, our first stop was lunch at La Terrace de Cojímar, a hangout of Ernest Hemmingway and Gregorio Fuentes, his first mate. The meal—paella with saffron rice in a creamy sauce with fish, shrimp, and a few cooked red pepper strips—was quite tasty. Hemmingway and his pals were known for frequenting this restaurant after fishing to down beers and hearty meals.

It is also the village where *Old Man and the Sea* is set. The laid-back town looks much as it did then, dusty and slightly rundown. Across the way, my view wandered to what looked like the remnants of a small Spanish fort known as the Torreón de Cojímar, another part of Havana's fortification system. Built in 1649 to protect the coast, the fortification managed to fend off the British fleet in 1762 though the Brits were able to land further up the coast.

The view of the coast utterly captivated me. I could have stared at the sea for hours and been perfectly content. No wonder Hemmingway stayed there twenty years. I mulled over the possibility of living there permanently as the sun streamed in through the open windows. The sea breeze was light and warm. Musicians strolled around strumming Cuban tunes. In my book, it was pretty much heaven on earth. I'm guessing if I lived there, I would be lulled into a daily nap after a *cerveza* or two. So relaxing. Those dreamy thoughts didn't last long, however.

Back on the bus, we headed about fifteen miles in from the coast to the port of Guanabacoa. This is not the happiest of places. Just like America, Cuba has a sordid history of slavery. In some ways, slavery in Cuba was worse because it started earlier and lasted longer. Spaniards and others began bringing Africans to work on Cuban sugar plantations as slaves in 1517. In fact, more Africans were brought to Cuba to work as slaves than were taken to America, Nilda said. I was astonished to hear this claim, but it turns out she was right.

D. R. Murray, a now retired University of Guelph history professor who has reviewed archival records, put the total number of Africans brought to Cuba and enslaved as close to 800,000. By contrast, Henry Louis Gates Jr., a Harvard professor, wrote in *The Root* that about 450,000 Africans were brought to the United States. Slavery wasn't abolished in Cuba until 1886, about twenty-three years after the Emancipation Proclamation took effect in the United States.

At Guanabacoa, we visited the Afro-Cuban Museum, a place that brings alive the impact of the enslaved Africans' religions on Cuban culture.

It's huge. Various expressions of African spiritual practices emerged and then fused with Catholicism over the centuries. Santería is just one of the African religious expressions that took root here.

Guanabacoa, the obligatory port of entry for slaves, became associated with West African cultures. At the Afro-Cuban Museum there, we learned about the Santeria religion. Here are three dancers right before they began an energetic dance swirling their colorful dresses.

Located in a beautifully restored colonial house, the public museum features a collection of revered spiritual figures known as *orichas* as well as costumes, religious objects, and musical instruments. We wandered around looking at showcases of objects. Then we were asked to sit on benches lining the wall in the interior patio. I began staring at a group of adorable school children on a field trip across the way. With their white shirts, red ties, and blue pants, they looked eager and excited. They reflected a rising anticipation in the room. Something unusual was about to happen.

The music began abruptly. It was loud and had a strong beat. Four dancers—three women and one man—emerged from a back hall. The women had on brightly colored floor-length dresses with matching headdresses. Each woman was dressed from head to toe in a different color—one red, one blue and one yellow. The man, who was slender and tall, was clad in red pants, a tight-fitting shirt and headdress. Slowly, they started twirling around. As the music picked up, they began whirling at a feverish pace all over the room. With skirts billowing, they seemed almost frantic. Their movements had no discernible pattern. They just seemed to move as the spirit called them to.

Suddenly, one dancer, known as a *Changa pricha*, approached one of my companions named Barbara. He stopped in front of her and stared. Then he danced. She told me afterward, "He was an imposing figure and a little intimidating. However, he noticed the brace on my arthritic knee and ministered to it. It did feel better afterward." A companion pointed out that her name tag, which read "Barbara," may have prompted him to pay special attention to her. Barbara is a patron saint of the Santeria. Though Afro-Cubans who practice Santeria know that Catholic saints and orichas are not identical, they see no problem keeping a statue of Saint Barbara on a Lucumí altar as another way of representing Changó, the African oricha of fire, lightning, and thunder.

CHAPTER 8

Only in Cuba

Though an estimated 65 percent of the population remains Catholic, only 5 percent or less attend church regularly. Up to 80 percent of the Cuban population has ties to Santería, estimates a US State Department report. Santería originated with the Yoruba, one of the African peoples brought to Cuba. Forced to practice Catholicism, the Africans incorporated their traditional beliefs into their new religion, so the two faiths exist side by side in what is commonly called "syncretism."

Practitioners of Santería may describe themselves as Catholic, attend Catholic masses, and baptize their children as Catholic but also practice their African-based religion in their own homes, a religious setting, or the home of a religious elder, according to aboutsanteria.com.

Many aspects of Afro-Cuban religion have been incorporated into the practice of Roman Catholicism in Cuba. The Black Madonna is worshipped at the cathedral known as Iglesia de Nuestra Señora de Regla in Havana.

On our way back to Havana's Hotel Melia Cohiba where we would stay that night, we stopped at the cathedral known as Iglesia de Nuestra Señora de Regla in Havana. Here we saw a statue of the Black Madonna prominently displayed in a small chapel. Venerated in the Catholic faith, she is the patron of fishermen and also associated with Santería. "The Catholic Church learned to be tolerant of the Santería religion," Nilda said. Cubans were praying at her feet. In many places around the world, Black Madonnas are associated with miracles. This wasn't a place that inspired me much.

But I was fascinated by the evolution of the Castros' views of the Catholic and Santeria religions. Immediately after the revolution, the government jailed priests, banned church leaders from the Communist Party, and seized church property, including the Jesuit school that Castro attended. Diehard Catholics found ways to celebrate their holidays and follow church teachings. One Cuban told us of a young person born in 1987 who was taken by his grandmother to the Catholic church to be baptized in secret so his parents could remain in the Communist Party.

Once Cuba lost the Soviet Union's economic support, more people turned to religion for solace, wrote Bret Sigler, a graduate journalism student at the University of California-Berkeley, in 2001 in a story posted on the UC-Berkeley Journalism School website.

"Sunday attendance rose at the few remaining churches and new ones opened," Sigler wrote. "Evangelical groups expanded and university students formed religious groups. Religion exploded and Castro retreated. He admitted in 1990 that the religious had been treated unjustly, and in 1992, the once atheist government declared itself a secular state and banned religious discrimination with an amendment to its constitution."

In 1998, Pope John Paul II made an historic visit to the island nation, which eventually led to Christmas becoming an official holiday. Fourteen years later, Pope Benedict XVI visited Cuba. Both Castros met with him. In May 2015, Raúl Castro visited Pope Francis in the Vatican to thank him for helping to broker the new relations with the United States. A few months later, the pope visited Cuba as well as the United States.

In early 2015, CNN reported that the first new Catholic church was set to be built since the 1959 revolution. The new church will be in Sandino, a small town in the country's western most provinces. "There is money to start, there is the construction material to start, there are the permissions to start, so everything is ready," Bishop Jorge Enrique Serpa Pérez, who oversees the diocese where the new church will be built, told CNN.

Socialism's Impact on Racism

In the pre-Castro era, racism played out much as it did in America. Private clubs and beaches were racially segregated. Even then President Batista, a mulatto, was denied membership in one of Havana's exclusive clubs, according to a 2004 PBS documentary. Mark Falcoff, an analyst quoted in the documentary, said: "One might best summarize the complex situation by saying that urban Cuba had come to resemble a southern European country (with a living standard as high or surpassing that of France, Spain, Portugal and Greece) while rural Cuba replicated the conditions of other plantation societies in Latin America and the Caribbean." For Nilda, those differences showed up when she was a university student. Havana natives made fun of her for being a *guajira*, a derogatory term for a female hillbilly.

Class differences and racial prejudice did not disappear when Castro came to power. But once Castro dismantled capitalism in the early 1960s and established egalitarian access to basic goods and services such as food, health, housing, employment, and education, Cuba came closer than any other country in this hemisphere to fulfilling economic justice, according to Alejandro de la Fuente, director of the Afro-Latin American Research Institute at Harvard University's Hutchins Center for African and African American Research.

By the 1980s, inequality by race had declined noticeably, he wrote. For example, the Cuban race gap in life expectancy was basically identical for all racial groups and significantly lower than those found in more affluent multiracial societies such as Brazil (about 6.7 years) and the United States (about 6.3 years) during the same period, he noted. "Racial differences in education and employment had also diminished or, in some cases, even disappeared," he wrote. "The proportion of high school graduates was actually higher among blacks than among whites in Cuba, whereas the opposite was true in both Brazil and the United States."

The statistics about Cuba's racial makeup are debated because intermarriage among all the racial groups makes almost no one purely white, black, or otherwise. And, as Nilda put it, "We have the African heritage even more than the Spanish heritage."

Nilda also made a point of showing us a March 8, 2013, story from *Bohemia*, which bills itself as the oldest magazine in Cuba. The piece featured pictures of members of the National Assembly. She said that 41.9 percent of the members were women, 38.6 percent black or mulatto, 61.3 percent were born after the revolution, and the average age of the body was fifty-seven. She did not tell us that only candidates who support the Castro regime are on the ballot.

Cuba's Racial Makeup
White: 64.1%
Black: 9.3%
Mulatto: 26.6%

Source: CIA World Book of Facts 2012 est.

Hmm, I thought, *even if the representatives are handpicked, someone apparently wants to reflect the diversity of Cuba's people or at least give the appearance that diversity is important.* Curious to see how the United States matched up, I found that the 114th US Congress is 80 percent white and 80 percent male, according to the *Washington Post.* And, of the 310 million Americans, 77.7 percent were white, and 48.8 percent were male in 2013.

Women in Cuba are paid the same as men for the same work and have equal access to jobs, Nilda told us. "Before the revolution, women were paid less for some work," she said. Cubans can vote when they turn sixteen and are supposed to wait until eighteen to consume alcohol or tobacco legally. But like youth in the United States, young people in Cuba widely disregard that law. Turns out teenagers' actions may be universal.

Gun-related violence is apparently nonexistent in Cuba. "We don't buy or sell weapons," she said. Cubans who commit a criminal act are assigned a government lawyer. If they're convicted and go to prison, they can take classes and earn degrees. The aim of prison is rehabilitation, not punishment, she said. Well, there's a contrast for you with the United States.

The United States–Cuba Clash

After Castro seized power, officials nationalized the homes, farms, oil refineries, factories, and other businesses of wealthy Cubans and Americans, most of whom fled the island. Today, some of these places are tourist attractions. We had a lovely dinner one night at Casa Espanola. Fashioned like a medieval castle, this was once the home of Gustavo Gutiérrez y Sánchez, Batista's finance minister, who was ridiculously wealthy judging from this place. Now the state-owned restaurant caters to tourists and is quite the showpiece.

Located in Miramar, a ritzy section of Havana, this home is ridiculously overdone, though I doubt its décor rivals Trump Tower and his gold-plated bathroom fixtures. With elaborately tiled ceilings and floors, the rooms have iron and rustic wooden furniture and medieval artifacts. Suits of armor lend a Don Quixote theme. Old rifles are affixed to the walls in one room. A domed stained-glass window depicting calla lilies adorns one vestibule. That alone is quite gorgeous.

As usual, they served us mojitos, a traditional Cuban cocktail consisting of white rum, sugar, lime juice, soda water, and mint, which were always good. Over a dinner of wine, chicken, and rice, I chatted with my colleagues about what we saw that day. The food was tasty but not remarkable. If anything, it was a bit bland—no interesting flavors. The conversation was much like the food. Most of my traveling companions did not express strong political opinions. They seemed to be there strictly as tourists. Perhaps they weren't willing to be openly critical of Castro's Cuba. Or maybe they were just too tired to engage in a political conversation. As for me, I was looking at this overdone splendor and thinking about how the money that built the place could have been better used on the Cuban people.

It's so sad to me that Fidel Castro lost his thirst for democracy and that US officials so badly misread the situation. Somehow, they thought Castro would succumb to US influence and power. The result has been a tit-for-tat relationship between the two countries ever since. When did relations start to deteriorate? Perhaps it was when the United States supplied arms and military advisers to Batista early on in his fight against Castro.

Though President Eisenhower recognized Castro as Cuba's leader shortly after Batista fled in 1959, Castro, by then, vowed to fight the United States. In 1960, Castro nationalized American-owned oil refineries in Cuba without providing compensation. In January 1961, the Unites States severed relations with Cuba and later imposed an embargo on exports to Cuba (except for food and medicine). In April of that year, a group of Cuban exiles backed by the CIA landed at the Bay of Pigs on Cuba's southern coast in an attempt to oust Castro. They were quickly squelched, a disaster for the United States that helped to cement Castro's power.

By February 1962, the embargo was expanded, and the United States pressured other countries to restrict trade with Cuba. Tensions rose again in October 1962 when Cuba allowed the Soviet Union to place medium-range ballistic missiles on the island, just ninety miles from Miami. Once the United States exposed the missiles, they were withdrawn in a face-saving deal that called for the United States to withdraw some of its missiles from Turkey. The resolution of this crisis that allowed me to go back to my happy life as a twelve-year-old required skilled diplomats and leaders who favored diplomacy and reason over bombastic, knee-jerk shows of force. Somehow, given Donald Trump's bombastic temperament and Vladimir Putin's sinister leanings, I feel the world is now less safe than ever.

Once Castro gained control, many Americans and Cubans who fled the island demanded reparations for their losses. Cuba has never paid any. Meanwhile, the US Congress authorized the Foreign Claims Settlement Commission, a quasi-government agency within the US Department of Justice, to review and validate claims of Americans. Deadlines for filing claims passed long ago. The commission validated nearly 6,000 of about 8,800 claims, totaling almost $2 billion. The *New York Times* reported the losses amount to $8 billion in today's dollars.

Cubans who later became American citizens were excluded from filing claims with the commission. However, now that United States-Cuba relations are on the mend, some experts believe Cuba may be open to resolving the reparations claims. But in January 2015, President Raúl Castro turned the tables and demanded reparations from the United States for losses incurred from the US trade embargo. In 1999, a Cuban court ruled that the United States owed Cuba $181 billion for damages from the embargo. That seems like a stretch. Perhaps he thinks he can gain some bargaining clout.

Nevertheless, the United States and Cuban officials met for the first time in Havana in December 2015 to exchange information on claims. By the end of Obama's presidency, nothing had been settled. And a continued stalemate seems most likely given Trump's hard-line stance on Cuba.

Even in his nineties, Fidel Castro was no fan of the United States. Shortly after his brother and President Obama announced the desire to reestablish diplomatic relations in 2014, the BBC reported that Fidel broke his silence in a letter published on the Cuban Communist Party newspaper, *Granma*. "I don't trust the policy of the United States ... but this does not mean I reject a pacific solution to the conflicts," he wrote. Once Fidel had stepped down as president, it was never clear how much, if any, impact he had on his brother's policy decisions.

Just as Fidel Castro's view didn't seem to change much, dissidents in Cuba have remained outspoken since he took power. In Castro's early years, dissidents were imprisoned and executed. In recent years, they have been detained and jailed. Despite the sordid past in curtailing Cubans' freedom of speech, several signs point to a more tolerant attitude toward dissidents. I was surprised when our tour bus drove by the Ladies in White, who protest the imprisonment of their husbands and others every Sunday. There they were, a line of ladies in white silently standing there.

The cynic in me wondered if the Cuban government wanted us to see that protests are tolerated in Cuba given that US news outlets occasionally report crackdowns on dissidents, mostly that they are jailed or held for hours just for expressing their views. But I find it interesting that President Obama spent almost two hours meeting with dissidents and civic leaders in the then newly reopened American embassy during his visit to Cuba in March 2016.

On Sunday, we passed the Ladies in White, a group of protestors started in 2003
by wives and other female relatives of jailed dissidents. The women protest each
Sunday by wearing white and walking silently through the streets.

CHAPTER 9

The Cuban Way

Midway through my trip, I began getting a glimpse of how ordinary Cubans negotiated their way through life. Before I arrived, I wondered whether a socialist government would thwart innovation. Years ago when traveling in other socialist countries, I noticed that service workers seemed bored and oblivious to the idea of customer service. Cubans were quite different. The waiters who served us and the vendors we encountered all seemed proud to do their jobs and attentive to our needs.

In fact, I believe the entrepreneurial spirit of Cubans thrives via a well-honed ability to solve the problems of everyday living with little or no money. As Nilda put it, "We always find a solution for everything. We call it the Cuban Solution."

For example, hitchhikers appear frequently on Havana's streets and roads, and Cubans who own cars pick up hitchhikers for a nominal fee. The practice fills in gaps for an inadequate public bus and train system. Though fares are low, buses become so packed with passengers that eventually they don't stop for additional riders on their routes.

The Cuban Solution also can be put another way: Cubans find a way to do what they're not supposed to do. In recent years, President Raúl Castro has allowed the establishment of private restaurants, known as *paladares*. We went to several during our trip. But these restaurants still operated with certain restrictions.

For example, government regulations prohibited the sale of beef and lobster outside of state-owned hotels and restaurants when I was there. Private restaurant owners could, if they went through a time-consuming bureaucratic process, get a permit to serve beef. Or they could purchase beef on the black market. Thus, while beef entrees may not be on the menu, chances are they have some if you ask.

The risk for Cubans is they can be fined if they are caught serving beef without a permit. But they have figured out a way around that, too. If confronted by a government official, they pull out a permit obtained long ago. And when the official notes the permit is very old, the restaurateur says the beef has been in the freezer and hasn't been used because demand is low. With a wink and a nod, that can be enough for an inspector to drop the matter.

One night, we dined at Il Divino, a private restaurant in Havana that opened in 2012. Located on four acres, the restaurant is surrounded by a botanical garden with a wide variety of trees whose genus and species were neatly marked with tags. Peacocks, parrots, and other birds roamed freely. Plans call for eventually serving meals to senior citizens, the owner told us.

Here is an inside view of Il Divino, a private restaurant in Havana known as a *paladare*. Opened in 2012, the restaurant sits on four acres surrounded by a botanical garden with a wide variety of trees. The genus and species were marked neatly with tags.

Inside, my group was seated at tables of four and six. Whitewashed walls with red tile floors provided a clean and attractive tropical feel to the place.

Attentive waiters served a delicious meal of chicken, rice, and vegetables. As I looked around, the place was busy and full of people who looked like tourists. I was judging mostly by racial and ethnic features. Americans tend to be a lot paler than most Cubans. But it's not always easy to distinguish between locals and tourists. Both groups dress alike, almost always in casual clothes. Men wear T-shirts and jeans. Women are clad in jeans or leggings and summer tops. The weather doesn't call for formal clothes here.

Private enterprise clearly seems to be gaining ground. One day, Nilda proudly announced: "We now have private property. We never knew what private property was." As an American, I found that idea hard to wrap my head around. My son is an entrepreneur who started his own business in 2002 and now has sixty employees. He's been far more successful than I ever was as a salaried worker during my earning years. Nilda seemed to embrace this newfound freedom, saying: "If you don't feel something belongs to you, you don't work as hard." Yet, she added that many Cubans remain skeptical that allowing legitimate private enterprise will improve their lives.

I wondered about that too when we visited a relatively new chocolate shop named Casa del Chocolat near our hotel in Santa Clara. Unlike an American candy shop, which is chock-full of choices for confections, this shop was about the size of a large elevator and had only one small display case of cakes, cookies, and candies. They were quite inexpensive by American standards. A lovely chocolate cake cost about eight dollars. I wish I could have bought it. Instead, we bought candies and shared them with our group. No one else was in the shop when we were there, making me wonder who the shop's customers were—tourists or locals? Could the average Cuban afford an occasional indulgence? I doubt it.

No Laughing Matter

Though some food staples, health care, and housing are subsidized, most families still don't earn enough to purchase many consumer goods. Many Cubans depend on relatives in America for extra cash. But even that is changing. Shortly after I returned in March 2014, the state-run newspaper, *Granma*, reported the wages of doctors with two specialties would go up to sixty-seven dollars a month from twenty-six dollars, while entry-level nurses would make twenty-five dollars, up from thirteen dollars a month.

Cubans' low wages hit home for me when I bought a necklace of shells from a vendor in a tourist market. After I paid for my purchase, the woman vendor asked me, "Do you have anything for me?" At first, I was baffled by what she meant. Slowly, she drew her finger across her lips as if putting on lipstick. Ah! She wanted lipstick. I dug into my purse and gave her a half-used tube. She smiled broadly and thanked me.

My traveling companions noticed the shortages too. We collected the travel-sized toiletries in our hotel rooms, which included shampoo and hand lotion. One day, we ventured several hours through the countryside when Nilda announced we were going to make a brief stop but for us to remain on the bus. The bus pulled to the side of the two-lane road. An older woman, lean with long, dark hair, stood there. Dressed in a light-colored blouse and dark skirt, she appeared to expect us. She took a few steps forward.

Nilda jumped off. The resemblance was striking. It was Nilda's mother, the woman who had created the kissing fairies. Embracing in a long and tight body hug, they remained entwined for several minutes. They talked. Her mother stroked Nilda's hair. Nilda gave her a plastic bag full of hotel toiletries we had collected, knowing such items are terribly expensive for Cubans. Embracing again, they parted as though they didn't want to let go of each other. Nilda rejoined us, and the bus moved on.

We visited a ration store where families can purchase a monthly allotment of some basic food, such as rice, chicken, eggs, coffee, and sugar at reduced prices. This store didn't seem very well stocked.

The food for sale in a ration store with the current prices.

A CUC store had well-stocked shelves full of many necessities, such as shampoo, cleaning products, and diapers, but these products generally are pricey for most Cubans.

Food is another mixed story. Each family has a ration booklet, or *Libreta de Abastecimiento,* that identifies every member of a household by age. With the booklet, families can purchase a monthly allotment of rice, sugar, oil, chicken, eggs, coffee, and other staples at the local ration store, or bodega, for a reduced rate. Items are weighed and sold in bulk. Some household goods, such as cooking fuels and cleaning products, also are distributed at these stores. We visited one near Vinales and saw sparsely stocked shelves.

Households with young children, nursing mothers, or elderly receive extra provisions. Rations are distributed only at the bodega that serves the area of their official residence. A person cannot receive rations from somewhere else without an official change of address, which is not easy to obtain.

A Cuban's Monthly Rations
- 10 pounds rice
- 3 pounds white sugar, 2 pounds brown sugar
- 1 pound cooking oil
- 1 pound dried beans
- 1 pound chicken
- 5 eggs

If young children are in the household, they can get powdered milk. Cigarettes no longer are part of monthly rations.

Cubans buy other goods at state-run stores, known as CUC stores, but they must use convertible pesos, known as CUCs (pronounced kooks). Typically, these stores offer a wider range and better quality of goods, such as cosmetics, paper products, and detergents. We stepped into one of these stores briefly. It resembled a small Target or Walgreens. Shelves were well stocked, but prices were high. A bag of thirty diapers cost three dollars, which would be a high proportion of the average twenty-five-dollars-a-month income.

As a consequence, a black market thrives in Cuba. Fernando Ravsberg, writing in the August 21, 2014, *Havana Times*, contended the black market exists because chronic shortages of everyday necessities have plagued Cubans for decades. "During the early years of the revolution, these shortages could be chalked up to the US embargo," he wrote.

Now, he asserted, Cuba's so-called planned economy is not well planned at all. Toilet paper can be unavailable, but pickled partridges can be stacked up on store shelves, he noted. "Cuba's entire distribution system is rotten," he wrote. "Importers are paid commissions, shopkeepers sell products under the counter, butchers steal and resell poultry, ration-store keepers mix pebbles in with beans, agricultural and livestock markets tamper with weighing scales and bakers take home the flour and oil."

Expensive Connections

Cubans also struggle to keep up with the modern world because they lack reliable and inexpensive access to the Internet. Currently, Internet access is expensive and spotty to nonexistent for most Cubans. One Cuban Solution is connecting to the Internet in the lobbies of hotels catering to foreigners.

At Meliá Cohíba Hotel, a five-star hotel facing the sea in Havana where I stayed, we saw several Cuban families in the corners of the lobby, where they pay five to fifteen dollars an hour. They were laughing and talking fast, presumably with their US relatives via their open laptops. As I was watching them, I wished I knew more Spanish so I could have understood what they were saying. I wondered if they simply exchange family news, or do they ever dare express politically contrary opinions in these conversations? The heavy-handed nature of an authoritarian government also became obvious here. Just a few decades ago, Cubans were not even allowed to go into hotels unless they worked there, Nilda told us. That prohibition, now lifted, was the government's crude attempt to prevent prostitution.

Since returning from Cuba, I learned that access to the Internet began loosening. By March 2015, a well-known sculptor named Kcho, who has close ties to the government, began offering free Internet access outside his Havana studio, the first free Wi-Fi spot in the country. A few months later, the Cuban government set up Wi-Fi hot spots that cost about two dollars an hour, the *New York Times* reported. And in 2016, President Obama also tried to improve Internet connections by exempting telecommunications equipment, technology, and services from the embargo. But even in 2017, Cubans still are a long ways from the seamless Internet connections that most Americans have in their daily lives. As Amnesty International noted in a press release issued right after Fidel Castro's death in November 2016, "The government continues to limit access to the Internet as a key way of controlling both access to information and freedom of expression. Only 25 percent of the Cuban population is able to get online and only 5 percent of homes have Internet access."

CHAPTER 10

Dr. Cuba

Health care in Cuba, on the other hand, has long been regarded as world-class. Even Amnesty International has acknowledged Castro's revolution for substantially improving access to health care. Despite limited resources and economic sanctions imposed by the United States for more than half a century, Cuba guarantees access to health care for all Cubans. Infant mortality rates are as good as or better than those of the United States, wrote Paul Drain, a Stanford physician, and Michele Barry, in a 2010 essay published in *Science*. "Not everything is perfect in Cuba," Drain told *Wired*. "There are shortages of medicines, and the best care is reserved for elites. But it's still a powerful feat." Cuba has one doctor for every 170 people, more than twice the US per-capita average.

Cubans have a right to ask for the doctor they want, Nilda said. Neighborhood health clinics make for easy access. And though health care is free, she said, Cubans often give small gifts to their doctors, such as food, soap, or sparkling wine. "It's not a bribe," she said. "You know they don't make much money. And they see every patient with a smile on their face."

Drain contends that America could learn a lot from the Cuban health care system. In 1964, the Cuban government began encouraging all medical school graduates to do at least two years of service in a rural area, he told *Wired*. The program became so popular that a decade later, almost all new doctors started in rural areas, focusing on primary care for all ages. "Once everybody learns primary care, about 35 percent go on and specialize," he said. "It's quite the opposite of what we have here."

He noted that in the United States, medical students choose their specialties, and only 7 or 8 percent go into family medicine. The resulting shortage of physicians in rural parts of the United States has been a longstanding problem. Medical students in Cuba also don't incur any debt from their schooling. The government pays the bill. In the United States, doctors completing their residencies have an average of $170,000 of debt, according to the Association of Medical Colleges.

In August 2014, an article in the *Huffington Post* quoted Margaret Chan, then the director-general of the World Health Organization, as saying: "Cuba is the only country that has a health care system closely linked to research and development. This is the way to go, because human health can only improve through innovation." She praised the country's leaders for making health an essential pillar of development.

The country continues to make important inroads to eliminating disease. In July 2015, the *New York Times* reported that Cuba became the world's first country to win World Health Organization certification after eliminating mother-to-child transmission of HIV and syphilis. Cuba successfully suppressed its HIV epidemic in the 1980s, first through forced quarantine, and since 1993 by widespread testing and treatment. To be certified by the WHO, a country must achieve 95 percent of elimination targets.

All of these achievements make me envious of Cuba's single-payer health care. The contrast is stark. With the byzantine US system, forty-five thousand Americans die each year for lack of insurance. The insurance industry remains in charge of life-or-death treatment decisions. Hospitals get away with charging $546 for six liters of saline that cost the hospital $5.16, according to one news report. And Big Pharma forces US consumers to pay ridiculously high drug prices. I just wish more Americans would wake up to the benefits of single-payer health care.

The Gay and the Bold

I was surprised one day when Nilda brought up the treatment of gays in Cuba. For years, homosexuality was considered immoral in Cuba. In the early days of Fidel Castro's regime, gays were ostracized, and some were sent to labor camps. The brutal treatment of gay men in Cuba was chronicled by Reinaldo Arenas, who was jailed in 1974 for literary works that authorities deemed an "ideological deviation." He wrote a critically acclaimed autobiography, *Before Night Falls*. And a 1993 Cuban film, *Strawberries and Chocolate*, which takes place in Havana in 1979, was nominated for an Academy Award in the best foreign film category in 1994.

Now, Nilda said, gender reassignment surgery is free, though gay marriage is not yet allowed. "But we're talking about it," she said. One current outspoken champion of gay rights in Cuba has been Raúl Castro's daughter Mariela, who is straight and heads the National Center for Sexual Education.

In 2007, Mariela led a small group of drag queens in an open demonstration. As the *New York Times* noted in a 2014 editorial, Ms. Castro "has carved out a rare space for civil society in an authoritarian country where grass-roots movements rarely succeed. Some Western diplomats in Havana have seen the progress on gay rights as a potential blueprint for expansion of other personal freedoms in one of the most oppressed societies on earth."

The *Times* credited her with persuading government officials to offer free gender reassignment surgery and hormone treatment in recent years. And last year, when the Assembly passed a law protecting gays and lesbians—but not transgender people—from discrimination in the workplace, Ms. Castro became the first lawmaker in Cuban history to cast a dissenting vote. As a Minnesotan, I was proud that my state legislature approved gay marriage in 2013. I don't see Cuba as being very far behind us here, and I can only hope that the US Supreme Court won't backtrack now that the Republicans have installed the fifth conservative vote.

CHAPTER 11

Food Irony

Toward the end of our tour, we headed out one last time from Havana. On this day, sunlight buttered the trees and shrubbery. The sky was a gorgeous bright blue, and the air was hot. The air-conditioning on the bus felt damn good. We were all downing water like parched camels. I was upbeat on our way to the Viñales Valley, the heart of Cuba's prime tobacco-growing region. Gradually, a feeling of disbelief swept over me. Hectare after hectare lay fallow. (One hectare equals about 2.47 acres.) We had seen similar expanses of unused land in other rural areas. Slowly, it dawned on me. The fallow ground was evidence that Cuba's agricultural policies had failed.

As one rural Cuban told us with some sadness, "We could produce anything we need to eat, but we import everything." For example, most of Cuba's chicken comes from the United States under a humanitarian agreement. In fact, 76 percent of Cuba's food is imported. How sad! Cuba is a country with a temperate climate and lengthy growing season. We could see that the land was uneven and might not be easy to farm. Small bushes and trees dotted large open spaces, but the land still looked as though the soil could be tilled. Certainly, it was nothing like the large, flat acres of rich black soil that we have in the US Midwest. Cuban soil is reddish brown. The only farm equipment we saw were old Russian tractors. More often, we saw oxen or horses pulling plows.

Cuba's inability to develop a robust, well-rounded agriculture sector dates back to the sixteenth century when sugar became the dominant export. Cuba first sold its sugar crop to Spain, then to the United States, and after the US embargo, to the Soviet Union. In 1991, the collapse of the Soviet Union ended the subsidies to Cuba. By then, Cuba was producing seven million tons of sugar a year and had 158 sugar processing plants. In 2014, there are forty-two. As Nilda put it, "Sugar has been our blessing and our curse. … You can't make soup with sugar."

In 2008, when international food prices spiked, President Raúl Castro expanded a program that provides free land to private farmers and cooperatives. Within a few months, nearly thirty-five thousand individuals or legal entities had applied, according to a story reprinted in the *Havana Journal* from the Cuban government's newspaper, *Granma.* About three-fourths of them had never farmed before. Forty-five percent of the applications were to raise cattle, and another 41 percent were for cultivating various crops.

Under this program, Cubans are limited to thirteen hectares or about thirty-three acres. "They don't want people to become large landowners," Nilda told us. That would never fly in Minnesota, where the average farm is 349 acres. Landholders who use all their land to produce eventually can expand their farms to about ninety-nine acres. Though new strategies to encourage more agricultural development are being adopted, some farmers remain skeptical. The agricultural ministry has earned a reputation of taking with one hand and giving with the other, we were told.

Under Castro, children helped harvest the crops. Nilda recalled working in the tobacco fields during her middle school years. On our road trip, we passed abandoned dormitories near old sugar plantations. With sugar production 40 percent of what it once was, many *compesinos,* or farm laborers, and their families moved to the cities in search of a better life. Many agriculture education programs also have ended because students aren't interested in them, Nilda told us. The shift has taken its toll. At one time, Cubans went to Vietnam to teach farmers how to grow coffee. Now the Vietnamese come to Cuba to teach Cubans how to grow it, she said. What a pity.

But I put all that unsettling reality aside as we approached the Viñales Valley, which is surrounded by the Sierra de los Organos mountain chain near the western end of the island. Listed as a Unesco World Heritage Site, the valley will fascinate any geology buff. Strange dome-like limestone hills, known as *mogotes,* rising as high as a thousand feet, dot the landscape. In the flat parts, peasant homes are surrounded by fields of tobacco, taro, and bananas.

Visiting a tobacco farm in the Vinales Valley was like stepping back to the early twentieth century. The farmer's home was small, cramped, and had few amenities.

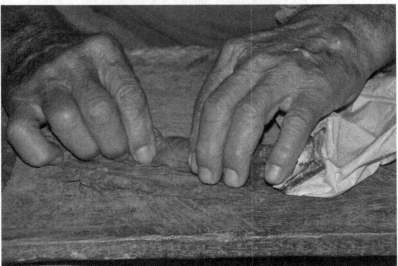

The grower, with his weathered face and stained hands, deftly rolled a cigar in minutes.

As we pulled onto a small dirt lane and headed toward a tobacco farm, I felt as though I could have been in a poverty-stricken part of rural Indiana or, worse yet, Appalachia. A small, one-story white house with blue trim and a red tile roof seemed right out of the early 1900s. The windows had only bars and wooden shutters, no glass. The whole place could have used a fresh coat of paint. Two Chevrolet coupes from the 1950s sat out back. The cars looked eerie to me in a way. My family had a car like that. I remember the back seats in those cars were huge. Or did it just seem that way because I was five?

Inside the house, an old upright piano nearly filled the tiny living room, which had rough-hewn walls with peeling paint. Dated photographs of older generations hung on the walls. The kitchen was a disaster. Buckets of water sat in the concrete sink lined with red tiles. I couldn't quite tell if that meant they had no running water. I didn't see a well outside. Two hot plates seemed to be the only means of cooking. They were sitting on a counter that had a huge crack below and exposed empty space underneath. Two small refrigerators—one with an Oakland A's sticker on the front— stood side by side. Various kitchen items sat on the tile counter. There were no cupboards. Taken aback, I didn't know whether to be impressed by the fact this farm was still operating, saddened by the dilapidated conditions, or simply thankful that it was a kind of living history tourist site.

After being served fruit drinks and cookies, we were ushered into a nearby building with a thatched roof. Rows and rows of tobacco leaves were hanging to dry from the low ceiling. An older worker with stained hands and a weatherworn face demonstrated how to roll a cigar. He did it deliberately. I think he slowed down the process so we could take it in. Later, I realized I had another feeling—one of a voyeur uncomfortable that all these tourists had invaded the home of these people and saw it in such dilapidated conditions. I just hope the owners made some money off the tourist buses that came through.

A young couple operates an organic farm in the Vinales Valley. They served us the best meal of the trip, which included roasted pig and a wide assortment of tasty dishes.

A short distance away, my spirits lifted when we arrived at an organic farm. We met the delightful young couple who ran it. They provided the best meal of the trip, by far. Seated in an outdoor area with a canopy, a light breeze, and a gorgeous view overlooking a valley, we started off with what was billed as an "antistress" cocktail. Laced with rum, this drink was a delicious, creamy concoction with coconut milk, pineapple, coconut, mint, basil, lemongrass, spearmint, cinnamon, and, of course, rum.

Fortunately, some of the women in my tour group asked for the recipe and shared it. The atmosphere was so charming that nearly everyone in my group was almost giddy as we were served a seeming endless array of well-prepared and flavorful food. Or could that have been the effects of the endless flow of rum, which was passed around in a bottle so we could add our own to our drinks.

Antistress Cocktail

1 small pineapple, chopped
2 tablespoons coconut milk (or coconut meat)
2 spoons of sugar (more if needed)
3 spoons of powdered milk
lemongrass, mint, basil, spearmint, anise, cinnamon
Cuban rum (white)

Blend pineapple, coconut milk, powdered milk, sugar, and ice in blender. It has to be thick. Add five herbs and blend again. Taste and add more sugar if needed. Serve in a glass with cinnamon sprinkled on top. Add rum and drink.

During the next few hours, we enjoyed *lechón asado* (roast pig), *moros y cristianos* (black beans and rice), *ajicao* (a stew of meat and vegetables), a soup of red peppers, yams, cabbage, and carrots, and a wide assortment of delicious side dishes that included plantains, fried corn and yams, cooked pumpkin slices, a salad of cucumbers and tomatoes. Various salsas were available to top off the vegetables. Delicioso!

Enthusiastic about their venture, the young farmers represent another face of a new Cuba. As Nilda translated, we learned that they had spent several years preparing the ground and building terraces for vegetable gardens on the gently sloping hillside of their property. They farm about seven hectares or seventeen acres. The soil is mostly clay, so they had to build up the nutrients with organic compost made of worms, manure, vegetables, and sawdust.

To control insects, they rely on marigolds, hibiscus, calla lilies, and sugarcane, he said. They also raise and sell chickens, pigs, and geese. They grow such vegetables as broccoli, cauliflower, and kale. But the young couple faces a problem also found in the United States. Cubans have a penchant for fried foods. They eat mostly rice, beans, and poultry. Green vegetables have not been a big part of their traditional diet.

Moreover, many fresh fruits and vegetables are expensive. The typical Cuban cuisine relies on pork, fowl, and rice—cooked with few spices— and tropical fruits. For now, the young couple caters to tourists and restaurants that attract Canadians and Europeans. Another busload of tourists was having lunch on the porch of the main house when we were there. Nevertheless, for this young couple to prosper, they will need a larger customer base that can afford and appreciate their produce.

After lunch, we made a brief stop at what I think was the worst tourist attraction in Cuba, the Mural de la Prehistoria. Commissioned by Fidel Castro in 1961, this 120-meter-high cliff art has been painted in garish colors that depict three humans, snails, a bull, and other animals. The artist, Leovigildo Gonzalez, was a student of the Mexican muralist, Diego Rivera. I'm sorry. I wish I could have liked it. I am a Rivera fan. This was one of the few times I felt I was in a tourist trap. Horse-riding hustlers didn't help with their aggressive efforts to be paid for having their pictures taken. I'm glad we didn't stay long.

Mecca of the Arts

A large part of our trip involved visiting arts and cultural organizations. I came to understand that Cuban culture offers a great deal of originality and distinctive art, more than I've seen in any other Caribbean country I have visited. I wondered why. The answer became clear once I discovered a genetic study that found Cuban ancestry to be 72 percent European, 20 percent African, and 8 percent Native American.

Cuba's unique mix of racial and ethnic identities has brought together the religions, music, arts, and foods of each group. This amalgam of customs and traditions, myths and legends play out in Cubans' daily lives. And nowhere is this mixed cultural heritage more obvious and fully expressed than in Cuban art, music, and literature. Indeed, artistic expression is ubiquitous, inescapable, and one of the joys of visiting the country.

I quickly became infatuated by all forms of Cuban artistic expression. During the week, we encountered dozens of artists, musicians, and dancers. Some were planned encounters. Others were spontaneous. At the Cuban Institute of Music, we heard a young man of about fifteen played a trumpet solo of "A Funny Valentine." It was haunting and poignant. The institute represents more than fifteen thousand professional musicians, who play all kinds of music, ranging from popular to jazz, pop to traditional and folk, salsa, rumba to classical.

Music is everywhere in Cuba. In the bars, at hotels, and at one rest stop we visited near Bacunayagua Bridge, the highest bridge in Cuba spanning a river of the same name. The music always makes me want to dance.

Live music is everywhere. We even encountered a four-piece musical group playing lively music at a rest stop along one highway. And after one lovely lunch of white fish, potatoes, and rice at the classy Café del Oriente just off the Plaza de San Francisco in Old Havana, my guy friend and I got up and danced to the American tunes they were playing. The musicians in the three-piece string group were delighted and urged us on. A few of our compatriots joined us, but the rest were too shy. I'm no great dancer, but

I couldn't help myself. Besides, I was burning a few calories. Although I thoroughly enjoyed myself, I have to admit to the cognitive dissonance of the experience of wondering whether an ordinary Cuban would ever be able to afford a meal in a place like that.

On another day, we stopped in at El Floridita, a historic fish restaurant and cocktail bar in the older part of Havana, where a waiter prepared the famous blue daiquiris said to be favored by Ernest Hemingway. We had an appetizer of tiny dried fish—crunchy but fishy tasting—and blue daiquiris made with Blue Curacao liqueur, apparently a favorite of Hemmingway's. But the highlight was the live band. The four-piece group included a striking jazz violinist with short-cropped red hair and large dangling earrings. The group, which also included a string bass, guitar, and bongo drums, had the place rocking, and this was in the middle of the day. Endorphins coursed through my body like a raging river. Hmmm, I guess the drinks didn't hurt either.

We also saw the Buena Vista Social Club—a Cuban group that gained worldwide fame in 1997 with a hit album—perform at one of our Havana hotels. Now, granted, some younger musicians had stepped in for some original group members who had died or retired. But the show was dazzling. Tickets were thirty dollars each and included appetizers. I couldn't believe how lucky I was to see them in Cuba.

At El Floridita, a historic fish restaurant and cocktail bar in the older part of Havana, a waiter prepares the famous daiquiris said to be favored by Ernest Hemingway.

Here is just one pretty and tasty meal we had. We ate in many lovely restaurants and hotels as well as some that were more common.

Cuban culture went through a major transformation once Castro took over. Under Batista, cultural organizations were privately supported and limited to Havana and, to a lesser extent, provincial capitals. On seizing power, Fidel Castro made arts readily available to the people. In 1959, he pumped $200,000 into the national ballet. Renamed the Ballet Nacional de Cuba, the company has become internationally known. And since then, the arts appear to be heavily subsidized by the government. But Castro's interest in the arts was not simply because he appreciated them or wanted to make them more accessible to ordinary Cubans. He used the arts to his own end.

"In an all-out effort to create a utopian Cuba, the arts were enlisted to play a crucial part," wrote Suki John, author of *Cuba: Contemporary Dance in Cuba: Tecnia Cubana as Revolutionary Movement*. "The ongoing tradition of Cuban dance, with African, Spanish and indigenous origins, made dance a logical tool for bringing together Cubans of varied backgrounds. ...

"The attempt to link to a national image with the visceral power of dance was a logical choice for a country with such strong dance lineage," she wrote. "Dance has played a large role in Cuban lives and self-concepts, contributing heartily to what is known as *cubanismo, cubanidad* or *cubania*—all of which loosely translate as 'Cuban-ness.'"

Che Guevara also embraced the role of the arts in a revolutionary society, John wrote. "He saw a need for supporting those Cuban artists who could speak to a population that varied greatly in education, culture and familiarity with the arts," she wrote.

In 1976, the Cuban Ministry of Culture formed a network of professional and amateur cultural organizations throughout the country. The ministry directs education programs in music, visual arts, ballet, dramatic arts, and modern dance, culminating in the university-level Higher Institute of Art. More than two hundred neighborhood cultural centers (*casas de cultura*) offer programs in all areas of the arts.

Professional organizations, unions, schools, and theaters also were established to train and present the new generation of artists to the masses. Today, the school associated with the ballet company, Escuela Nacional Cubana de Ballet, has three thousand students and is billed as the largest in the world. Specialized schools start at the elementary school level and lead to advanced education in such fields as music, painting, sculpture, dance, ballet, and the performing arts.

The Cuban government's emphasis on the arts stands in sharp contrast to the way the arts are viewed in the United States. Often, funding for arts education and programs is cut in hard times. Public elementary schools in Saint Paul, Minnesota, recently eliminated music classes. Unbelievable! And now the United States has a president who wants to drastically slash or eliminate funding to the National Endowment for the Arts and the Public Broadcasting System. To me, that's almost a criminal act. That's like cutting the soul out of a country. Yes, the United States has its specialized schools, such as Julliard, but at best, America's system for producing a new generation of artists is spotty and open mostly to the privileged few. In Cuba, talent seems to be the determining factor.

Seeing members of the Contemporary Dance Company of Cuba demonstrate various hip, torso, and hand movements in *la técnica cubana* was enlightening and impressive. Contemporary Cuban dancing combines modern American theatre, Afro-Caribbean dance styles, and classical European ballet. Founded in 1959 by Ramiro Guerra, who had danced with Martha Graham's company in New York, the company draws sixty or so members from the Escuela Nacional de Arte. The troupe has toured all over the world. For a taste of what they do, see http://havana-cultura.com/en/performing-arts/danza-contemporanea-de-cuba.

We also visited the unbelievable home and studio of Jose Rodriquez Fuster. Regarded as the Picasso of the Caribbean, Fuster lives in Jaimanitas, a suburb of Havana. Brightly colored ceramic murals and sculptures, often of whimsical sea creatures, cover nearly every inch of the walls, roofs, hallways, benches, doorways, fountains, and archways of his house. His work extends to the homes of more than eighty neighbors. The work of a lifetime is right before your eyes. The display is quite dazzling.

Jose Rodrigues Fuster, known as the Picasso of the Caribbean, has covered his house and his neighbors' houses with ornate ceramic murals. He lives in a suburb of Havana and has decorated more than eighty houses with the ceramic murals to suit the personalities of his neighbors.

My traveling companions seemed surprised that Cubans could make a living as professional musicians or artists. After one performance, one of my companions asked a musician, "What do you for a living?" The perplexed musician replied, "Play music seven days a week." Doing so is not seen as risky or less useful in Cuba, as it often is in the United States.

To be fair, Cuba's artists and musicians may be able to earn a livelihood, in part, because wages are low for nearly everyone, thus artists don't seem poorer than anyone else. Admission to concerts, museums, dance performances, and the like is affordable for most Cubans, costing as little as fifty cents. By contrast, tickets are hundreds of dollars for our rock stars.

CHAPTER 12

Yank Tanks and Me

Of course, no trip to Cuba would be complete without riding in one of the 1950s-era American cars. The surprise for me was there were so many. Hundreds of these old American gems fill the streets of Havana and elsewhere. By one estimate, there are sixty-five thousand vintage cars on Cuban roads. Some are in stellar condition. Others, not so much. The early 1950s Chevys and Fords seem to be the most common, though Buicks, Plymouths, and Oldsmobiles are around, too. Every once in a while, I spotted a Cadillac. Nilda explained that some of these cars have had their outsides restored and their insides replaced with new parts or Toyota engines. Occasionally, we saw a Moskvitch 2141, a boxy little Soviet-era number that arrived in Cuba in 1986.

Cars were another area in which the Castros exerted authority. For nearly fifty-five years, Cubans could only purchase cars made before 1959 without a permit. In January 2014, Raúl Castro began allowing Cubans to buy new and used cars without a permit. Prices, however, were out of reach for most Cubans. Only fifty cars and four motorcycles were purchased in the first six months. The average sale price of the vehicles was $23,800, the *Havana Times* reported in July 2014.

By now, "Yank tanks" have become part of Cuba's brand and provide a particular pleasure for American tourists. Just looking at them transported me to my youth in the fifties. I pictured riding in one. On the last full day of our tour, my wish came true. Our group rented eight 1950s-era cars in excellent condition. It didn't hurt that they were convertibles and the day was gorgeous. I scrambled to jump into a hot pink 1956 Ford Fairlane convertible with white leather interior. Oh-la-la! Though I picked the car for the color, the driver was definitely "mango"—a slim but muscular body with gorgeous golden-brown skin and sporting a black cowboy hat. We took off.

All eight cars tooled along the *malecón*, the main drag along the Havana harbor for about two hours, at about forty miles per hour. The warm sun bathed my face. The wind whipped through my hair. I felt like a slaphappy teenager from *Happy Days*, that popular American sitcom about life in the fifties. My companions were just as giddy. We shrieked. We shouted. We waved. The drivers honked. The cars played tag with each other. It was an exhilarating experience. The shock came once the ride was over. One of my traveling companions pointed out that the cars had no seat belts. I had forgotten all about seat belts. I couldn't believe how quickly I adjusted to being in a car without seat belts—an act that is unthinkable for me at home. I have to admit that I didn't miss them.

But I also was vaguely cognizant during that joy ride that here was one more example of two Cubas—one for tourists and one for the Cubans. Here I was, a "rich" American who could play like a child. Yet my driver would have to work seven lifetimes to earn what I had during my lifetime.

Conclusions

In 2017, I began to ponder how this trip to Cuba had changed me and my views of my own country as well as Cuba. Right now, living in Cuba doesn't look half bad. While Cuba reminds me of a mango—sweet and succulent with a firm flesh and a hard core—America seems more like a prickly pear, a largely unknown fruit that grows erratically and has pads protruding at all angles with barbed spines. For me, this fruit symbolizes the largely hidden mass of discontented Americans, the factions within our political parties poking out in all directions, and the barbs of crude, rude, and hateful racist, anti-Semitic discourse that fills social media and extreme right-wing "news" outlets. No wonder we avoid political discussions with anyone but those in our own camp. Meanwhile, the infamous top 1 percent continues to amass political power, and the rest of us worry about losing what we have and any sense of a secure future for our children and grandchildren. But even the prickly pear offers colorful blooms and a luscious fruit. So I will not be discouraged by the mangled state of America's democracy right now, and I will continue to stand for a democracy and an economy that works for everyone.

As for Cuba, I can see I was unaware that I had harbored such deep-seated opinions of Cubans as generally less worldly and less sophisticated than most Americans. Boy, is that rubbish. In short, I saw an "arrogant American" side of myself that I do not like and still do not want to recognize. My encounters with Cubans were like a splash of cold water in my face. Many Cubans I met were in tune with what was happening in America. They enjoy the same entertainment and, for all I know, are more in touch with the rest of the world than I am.

I worry about what will happen to Cuba once the travel ban is fully lifted, which is inevitable in my opinion, even if it doesn't happen with Trump. Harriet Alexander, a foreign correspondent for the *Daily Telegraph* in the UK, put it best shortly after Presidents Obama and Raúl Castro announced a renewal of diplomatic relations: "Will the island now be subject to an invasion of US cruise ship passengers, and college students on spring break bacchanals? ... Part of the magic of the island is its sense of being lost in time—a country where billboards advertise loyalty to Fidel Castro rather than the latest Nike shoe, and where the traffic is a brightly coloured convoy of 1950s Studebakers, Chevrolets and Oldsmobiles. The risk now is that these emblems of a faded world, if they are preserved at all, will only form a theme-park attraction for the very tourists whose arrival spelled their doom."

Though I entered Cuba with a favorable attitude toward Cubans, my admiration grew exponentially each day of my visit. I have a much deeper appreciation of their distinctive, rich, and complex culture. I am humbled and awestruck that despite fifty plus years of hardships, the spirit of the Cuban people seems indefatigable. I found Cubans to be vibrant, optimistic, hospitable, engaging, modest, and charismatic. The Cuban character, if there is such a thing, charmed me. I loved the irreverent self-deprecating sense of humor. And to tell the truth, I am a bit envious. In my interactions, they generated hope for a stronger and better Cuba, exuded an appreciation for what they had, and expressed nothing but friendship for Americans.

The Cubans' openness to Americans stands in sharp contrast to the many Americans who currently seem closed to welcoming new immigrants. I find this American nationalism terribly disheartening. Yet I do wonder whether I saw a varnished picture of life in Cuba. I know hundreds, if not thousands, of Cubans still want to come to America every year. Why? I didn't encounter anyone who seemed unhappy or harshly criticized the government. I wish I had asked more questions of the Cubans I met about why some of their fellow citizens want to flee.

I also came away believing that Cubans seem to appreciate life more intensely, particularly for the simple things, than Americans seem to do. Is it because the hardships have put the miracle of life in perspective? Is it because Cuba has a temperate climate, beautiful beaches, and gorgeous sunsets within everyone's reach? Or is it because they live amid a plethora of historic landmarks that instill pride and a sense of durability? Plentiful mangoes and avocados also must provide untold pleasure. They would for me, anyway. The abundance of creative expression in Cuba—from the performing arts to the fine arts—also surely must nourish and sustain their spirits even through tough times. Every time I was around the musicians, my spirits soared.

On the other hand, seeing the toll firsthand that the longstanding intransigence of the US and Cuban governments has taken on the Cuban people was heart-wrenching. Now as I picture the Cubans I met and the price they paid, I'm saddened, angry, and even feeling guilty for my storybook life. Their economy was severely damaged, if not destroyed. They have remained mired in outdated means of communication and economic production. They have been forced to focus on survival, rather than growth and prosperity.

It seems as though our two countries have been locked in a standoff for five decades fixated on the idea that the other country has it all wrong. Consequently, the tit-for-tat affronts that have occurred over the last five decades seem so childish now. Take the time that the United States put a sign that urged Cubans to leave Cuba on top of the building housing the "US Interests Section," America's de facto embassy in Havana until the US embassy reopened in July 2015. It's embarrassing.

In response, Cuban officials installed a few dozen flagpoles and displayed black flags on a roof nearby to symbolize the people who had died fleeing Cuba. Subsequently, America removed the sign. And Cuba took down the flags, which were causing complaints because of the noise from the flapping flags. As Nilda noted when we drove by what is now the US embassy, "Where there's an action, there's a reaction."

Such realities are not lost on the Cuban people. Like Americans, Cubans have a healthy skepticism of their government. I was surprised by the Cubans' willingness to complain about their government. Their complaints even seem laughingly familiar: a bureaucracy that is inefficient and slow. They talked of failed policies and unmet expectations. At one point, I asked a Cuban, "Could you get in trouble for what you said?" Yes was the reply. Another Cuban summed it up by saying, "The feeling in Cuba is not rebellion. The feeling in Cuba is mostly disappointment."

I recognize now that I entered Cuba with a great deal of discomfort about my ambivalent views. Here's where the personal becomes the political. How does one admire and dislike Fidel Castro at the same time? How does one support lifting the US embargo without letting the Cuban government off the hook for its human rights violations? How does one reconcile the losses incurred by Cubans who fled the island when Fidel Castro seized power with the universal health care and education he put in place that raised the living standards of most Cubans?

Of course, the ham-handed actions of Cuban officials have held back the country's economy and restricted Cubans' rights to life, liberty, and the pursuit of happiness too. But I have to conclude that the United States, as the Goliath, harmed the Cuban people more than their own government's actions. And the irony is that the United States didn't "win," either. The United States forfeited $1.2 billion a year in lost trade with Cuba, according to the *Harvard Political Review*. And now that the European Union negotiated a deal with Cuba in 2016 that includes cooperating on trade and engaging in a dialogue on human rights, American businesses stand to lose out even more.

So here we are in mid-2017. A small contingent of American politicians still opposes lifting the US trade embargo despite overwhelming support among Americans for ending the ban. During the campaign, President Trump vowed to roll back Obama overtures to Cuba. But we have seen how Trump talked tough about China, NATO, and South Korea and then—in true Trump style—moderated his view. As of May 2017, a White House review of American policy toward Cuba is still underway. What baffles me is why President Trump, a business guy always looking to make a buck, would prevent American businesses from moneymaking opportunities in Cuba.

If he holds firm to his original promise, he is harming American farmers and businesses by preventing access to a new market. The entire Minnesota congressional delegation, which includes three Republicans in largely rural districts, favors lifting the trade embargo. And, as a recent Brookings Institution report on tourism in Cuba noted, "… it is contradictory to allow a surge in US visitors without allowing US business to help to construct the infrastructure required to receive those visitors and to provide them with a secure and comfortable sojourn. The Obama administration allowed US firms to sell to projects that 'benefit the Cuban people.' It is now time to permit US firms to participate in projects that also benefit the American people, as visitors to Cuba." Here, here, I say.

In some ways, it seems so simple. Americans and Cubans should be natural allies. We are neighbors, for God's sake. Our histories have been intertwined for centuries. Our cultures have fed off each other, often for the better. In essence, each country complements and broadens the other. But we get hung up by stupid politics.

Most of the American hostility toward Cuba lies with the fact that it is a dictatorship, not a democracy. Cubans cannot speak freely, govern themselves through truly democratic elections, and pursue their dreams in a free enterprise system. They struggle to buy goods and services beyond necessities, even though they have free or subsidized food, housing, and health care.

Throughout my trip, I mulled the costs and benefits of capitalism versus socialism. Cuba is unable to take advantage of capitalism's benefits—innovation, efficiency, political and economic freedom—and has yet to overcome socialism's drawbacks, which include slower economic growth, less technological advancement, less consumer freedom, and greater inefficiency. Meanwhile, socialism's virtues—a safety net for all that provides health care and education—seem to be scorned in the United States despite Bernie Sanders's popularity. And Americans suffer from its disadvantages—economic inequality, monopolistic practices, price gouging, and undermining of health, education, and the environment. In short, neither system seems to have a lock on the best way to ensure economic prosperity, liberty, and justice for all.

At the same time, it's difficult to separate the benefits of Cuba's socialism from a political structure that suppresses free speech, abuses dissidents, and imposes dictatorial mandates. Likewise, Cubans may have a hard time separating America's democracy from the cannibalistic nature of its capitalistic system.

Whoever is to blame for the damages caused by the contentious relationship, one thing is clear to me: unreliable access to the Internet and fields plowed by oxen do not a modern country make. America can and should help bring Cuba into the twenty-first century.

A new era between Cuba and the United States is upon us, whether we like it or not. Our two peoples have much to learn from each other. And I dare to say that Americans have more to learn from Cubans than vice versa. We seem to have lost the ability to respect those who disagree with us in America. From everything I saw, various factions within Cuba seem to respect one another. Perhaps Cubans can help us regain that.

We must allow our opposing views to coexist. It doesn't mean Americans must give up standing for basic human rights and the possibility of Cuba becoming a fully developed democracy. And it doesn't mean Cuba must adopt capitalism. What I would love to see is for each country to blend the best aspects of capitalism and the best aspects of socialism.

What lies ahead for Cuba-America relations? In the end, I assert that it will be our two peoples—rather than our governments—that will overcome our differences. We simply must demand that our politicians understand it is in the best interests of Americans and Cubans to embrace what works best in each other's countries and raise the bar for prosperity and full self-expression for everyone. With that mandate, Cuba and the United States really could be best of friends.

Melinda Voss, the author, at the Il Divino courtyard.

BIBLIOGRAPHY AND NOTES

Chapter 1

Hanson, Daniel, Dayne Batten, and Harrison Ealey. "It's Time for the U.S. to End Its Senseless Embargo of Cuba." *Forbes*, January 16, 2013. Accessed September 6, 2016.

http://www.forbes.com/sites/realspin/2013/01/16/its-time-for-the-u-s-to-end-its-senseless-embargo-of-cuba/#3c3211615430.

Hudson, Rex A. "Cuba: a country study." Federal Research Division, Library of Congress. 2001. Accessed September 6, 2016. https://cdn.loc.gov/master/frd/frdcstdy/cu/cubacountrystudy00huds/cubacountrystudy00huds.pdf.

McCannon, Aili. "Havana Gets a Face-Lift." *New York Times*, May 10, 2017.

Chapter 2

Hamberg, Jill. "Cuba Opens to Private Housing but Preserves Housing Rights." *Race, Poverty and the Environment Journal* 19 (2012). Accessed September 8, 2016. http://www.reimaginerpe.org/node/6930.

Kre-pi, Bill. *Cultural Sociology of Divorce: An Encyclopedia*, edited by Robert E. Emery, 331–333. Sage Publications Inc., 2013. Accessed September 8, 2016. https://books.google.com/books?id=ix9zAwAAQBAJ&pg=PA332&lpg=PA332&dq=Cultural+Sociology+of+Divorce:+An+Encyclopedia+Cuba&source=bl&ots=wQcKDsiL4v&sig=axZnVdBXYOnfELARRaY0i5FZ59U&hl=en&sa=X&ved=0ahUKEwjD3rwx4DPAh

VG1B4KHfLAC8sQ6AEINzAD#v=onepage&q=Cultural%20
Sociology%20of%20Divorce%3A%20An%20Encyclopedia%20
Cuba&f=false.

Moreno, Rogelio Manuel Diaz. "Cuba's Divisive CDR Defense
Committees." *Havana Times,* September 26, 2014. Accessed September
8, 2016. http://www.havanatimes.org/?p=106368.

Peters, Philip. "Cuba's New Real Estate Market," Brookings Institution,
February 2014.

Chapter 3

"Old Havana and its Fortification System," UNESCO World Heritage
Centre. Accessed September 8, 2016. http://whc.unesco.org/en/
list/204.

"Pre-Castro Cuba*," PBS American Experience.* Accessed September 8, 2016.
http://www.pbs.org/wgbh/amex/castro/peopleevents/e_precastro.
html.

Chapter 4

Broadle, Anthony. "Castro: Cuba not cashing US Guantanamo rent
checks," *Reuters*, August 17, 2007. Accessed September 6, 2016. http://
www.reuters.com/article/2007/08/17/idUSN17200921.

Bruns, Barbara, Javier Luque, et al. "Great Teachers: How to Raise
Student Learning in Latin America and the Caribbean." *World Bank*,
11. 2014. Accessed September 24, 2016. http://www.worldbank.
org/content/dam/Worldbank/document/LAC/Great_Teachers-
How_to_Raise_Student_Learning-Barbara-Bruns-Advance%20
Edition.pdf.

Delgado, Elio. "Cuban Education: A State Responsibility." *Havana
Times*, September 7, 2012. Accessed September 19, 2016. http://www.
havanatimes.org/?p=78108.

Flynn-Schneider, Andrea. "Human Rights Situation of Persons with
Disabilities in Cuba." *Human Rights Brief,* March 29, 2014. American
University Washington College of Law Center for Human Rights &
Humanitarian Law. Accessed September 19, 2016. http://hrbrief.org/
hearings/human-rights-situation-of-persons-with-disabilities-in-cuba/.

"History of Cuba." *Wikipedia.* Accessed September 6, 2016. https:// en.wikipedia.org/wiki/History_of_Cuba.

"Old Havana and its Fortification System." World Heritage Site, UNESCO. Accessed September 19, 2016. http://whc.unesco.org/en/list/204.

"Pre-Castro Cuba." *PBS American Experience.* Accessed September 8, 2016. http://www.pbs.org/wgbh/amex/castro/peopleevents/e_precastro. html.

Ravsberg, Fernando. "Cuba's Educational System Needs New Investment." *Havana Times,* September 3, 2015. Accessed September 19, 2016. http://www.havanatimes.org/?p=113695.

Chapter 5

Fagen, Richard. "Cuba and the Soviet Union." *Wilson Quarterly* (Winter 1978). Accessed April 25, 2017. http://archive.wilsonquarterly.com/ sites/default/files/articles/WQ_VOL2_W_1978_Article_01_2.pdf.

Garrison, Laura Turner. "The Cuban Comedy (Non-)Crisis." *Splitsider,* January 25, 2012. Accessed September 8, 2016. http://splitsider. com/2012/01/the-cuban-comedy-non-crisis/.

Gorry, Conner. "Conner's Cuba Rules Part II." *Here is Havana Blog,* June 24, 2012. Accessed September 8, 2016. https://hereishavana.com/.

Chapter 6

Krauze, Enrique. "Cuba: The New Opening," *New York Review of Books,* April 2, 2015. Accessed March 25, 2015. http://www.nybooks.com/ issues/2015/04/02/.

Whitefield, Mimi. "Venezuelan oil might be behind Cuba's pivot to the U.S." *Miami Herald,* December 18, 2014. Accessed September 24, 2016. http://www.miamiherald.com/news/nation-world/world/ americas/cuba/article4651707.html.

Chapter 7

Dominquez, Jorge I. *Cuba: Order and Revolution.* Belknap Press, 1978. Accessed September 6, 2016. https://en.wikipedia.org/wiki/Cuba.

Olson, James Stuart. *Historical Dictionary of the 1950s,* 67–68. Greenwood Publishing Group, 2000. Accessed September 6, 2016. https:// en.wikipedia.org/wiki/Cuba.

"Religion in Cuba." *Wikipedia.* Accessed September 14, 2016. https:// en.wikipedia.org/wiki/Religion_in_Cuba.

Sanderlin, Terry K. *The Last American Rebel in Cuba.* AuthorHouse, 2012. Accessed September 6, 2016. https://en.wikipedia.org/wiki/Cuba.

Sigler, Bret. "Saving the Cuban Soul," *Cubans 2001.* University of California Berkeley School of Journalism. Accessed September 19, 2016. http:// journalism.berkeley.edu/projects/cubans2001/story-religion.html.

Oppmann, Patrick. "Cuba to build first new Catholic Church since Castro." *CNN,* January 30, 2015. Accessed September 19, 2016. http:// edition.cnn.com/2015/01/30/living/cuba-catholic-church/index.html.

"Why is it Called Santeria." *About Santeria.* Accessed September 19, 2016. http://www.aboutsanteria.com/what-is-santeria.html.

Chapter 8

"An aging population will test Cuba's economic reform." *Jamaica Observer,* August 8, 2012. Accessed September 19, 2016. http://www.jamaicaobserver.com/pfversion/ An-aging-population-will-test-Cuba-s-economic-reform_12218294.

Completed Programs, Foreign Claims Settlement Commission of the United States, US Department of Justice. Accessed September 8, 2016. https://www.justice.gov/fcsc/claims-against-cuba.

"Danzón." Wikipedia. Accessed September 24, 2016. https://en.wikipedia. org/wiki/Danz%C3%B3n#cite_ref-Urf.C3.A9_1965_1-0.

English, J.T. *Havana Nocturne: How the Mob Owned Cuba and Then Lost It to the Revolution.* William Morrow, 2008. Accessed September 6, 2016. https://en.wikipedia.org/wiki/Cuba.

Guerra, Lillian. "Beyond Paradox: Counterrevolution and the Origins of Political Culture in the Cuban Revolution, 1959–2009." In *A Century of Revolution. American Encounters/Global Interactions,* edited by Greg Grandin and Gilbert M. Joseph, 199–238. Durham, NC: Duke University Press, 2010. Accessed September 6, 2016. https:// en.wikipedia.org/wiki/Cuba.

Guerra, Lillian. *Visions of Power in Cuba: Revolution, Redemption, and Resistance, 1959–1971,* 122. Chapel Hill: University of North Carolina Press, 2012. Accessed September 6, 2016. https://en.wikipedia.org/ wiki/Cuba.

Gates Jr., Henry Louis. "How many slaves landed in the US," *The Root*, January 6, 2014. Accessed August 12, 2016. http://www.theroot.com/articles/history/2014/01/how_many_slaves_came_to_america_fact_vs_fiction/.

Murray, D. R. "The Slave Trade and Slavery in Latin America and the Caribbean." *Latin American Research Review* 21 (1986): 202–215. Accessed January 19, 2016. http://www.jstor.org/stable/2503510.

Robles, Frances. "In Talks Over Seized U.S. Property, Havana Counters with Own Claim," *New York Times*, December 13, 2015. Accessed September 8, 2016. http://www.nytimes.com/2015/12/14/world/americas/talks-begin-in-cuba-on-confiscated-us-property-worth-billions.html?_r=0.

Rosenberg, Jennifer. "Who was Fidel Castro." About.com. Accessed September 8, 2016. http://history1900s.about.com/od/people/p/castro.htm.

Wickham-Crowley, Timothy P. *Exploring Revolution: Essays on Latin American Insurgency and Revolutionary Theory*, 63. Armonk, NY, and London: M.E. Sharpe, Inc., 1990. Accessed September 6, 2016. https://en.wikipedia.org/wiki/Cuba.

Chapter 9

De La Fuente, Alejandro. "A Lesson from Cuba." *New York Times*, November 17, 2013. Accessed September 14, 2016. http://opinionator.blogs.nytimes.com/2013/11/17/a-lesson-from-cuba-on-race/?_r=0.

"Rationing in Cuba." *Wikipedia*. Accessed September 24, 2016. https://en.wikipedia.org/wiki/Rationing_in_Cuba.

Ravsberg, Fernando. "The Causes and Consequences of Cuba's Black Market." *Havana Times*, August 21, 2014. Accessed September 8, 2016. http://www.havanatimes.org/?p=105653.

Siegel, Robert. "An Object Of Desire: Hope And Yearning For The Internet In Cuba," *National Public Radio*, March 23, 2015. Accessed September 8, 2016. http://www.npr.org/sections/parallels/2015/03/23/394276385/an-object-of-desire-hope-and-yearning-for-the-internet-in-cuba.

Chapter 10

"A Castro breaks tradition with 'no' vote in Cuba," Associated Press and Al Jazeera, August 19, 2014. Accessed September 24, 2016. http://america. aljazeera.com/articles/2014/8/19/castro-cuba-parliament.html.

"Cuba's Gay Rights Evolution." *New York Times*, December 20, 2014. Accessed September 19, 2016. http://www.nytimes.com/2014/12/21/ opinion/sunday/cubas-gay-rights-evolution.html.

Drain, Paul K., and Michele Barry. "Fifty Years of U.S. Embargo: Cuba's Health Outcomes and Lessons." *Science* 328, no. 5977 (April 30, 2010).

Keim, Brandon. "What Cuba Can Teach Us About Health Care." *Wired*, April 29, 2010. Accessed September 19, 2016. https://www.wired. com/2010/04/cuban-health-lessons/.

Lamrani, Sallim. "Cuba's Health Care System: a Model for the World." *Huffington Post*, August 8, 2014. Accessed September 19, 2016. http://www.huffingtonpost.com/salim-lamrani/cubas-health-care-system-_b_5649968.html.

McNeil Jr., Donald G. "Cuba Wins W.H.O. Certification It Ended Mother-to-Child H.I.V. Transmission." *New York Times*, June 30, 2015. Accessed September 19, 2016. http://www.nytimes.com/2015/07/01/ health/who-certifies-end-of-mother-to-child-transmission-of-hiv-in-cuba.html?_r=0.

Pages, Raisa. "Tens of Thousands of Cubans apply to cultivate Cuban farm land." *Granma*, Oct. 7, 2008. Accessed September 19, 2016. http://havanajournal.com/business/entry/ tens-of-thousands-of-cubans-apply-to-cultivate-cuban-farm-land/.

Chapter 11

"Cuba: Cultural Life." *Encyclopedia Britannica*. Accessed September 19, 2016. https://www.britannica.com/place/Cuba/Cultural-life.

"Cuban National Ballet." Wikipedia. Accessed September 19, 2016. https:// en.wikipedia.org/wiki/Cuban_National_Ballet.

John, Suki. *Contemporary Dance in Cuba: Tecnia Cubana asRevolutionary Movement*. McFarland, 2012. Accessed September 19, 2016. https:// books.google.com/books?id=drE0KI3h7UC&pg=PA5&lpg= PA5&dq=Cuba:+Contemporary+Dance+in+Cuba:+Tecnia+

Cubana+as+Revolutionary+Movement.&source=bl&ots=wBf6RXa
___4&sig=veaHepnKUP2hhyIkoYc59i4il4&hl=en&sa=
X&ved=0ahUKEwjIipT5pZzPAhVJ34MKHULRBZwQ6AEIP
TAG#v=onepage&q&f=false.

Chapter 12

Alexander, Harriet. "After years in the time warp, Cuba faces a new revolution." *Daily Telegraph*, December 20, 2014. Accessed September 24, 2016. http://www.nzherald.co.nz/business/news/article.cfm?c_id=3&objectid=11376994.

"Cuba Car Sales Fail over Sky High Prices." *Havana Times*, July 1, 2014. Accessed September 19, 2016. http://www.havanatimes.org/?p=104581.

Londoño, Ernesto. "Cuban Dissidents Buoyed in a New Era." *New York Times*, August 24, 2015. Accessed August 24, 2015. http://www.nytimes.com/2015/08/24/opinion/cuban-dissidents-buoyed-in-a-new-era.html.

Marcheco-Teruel, B., et al. "Cuba: Exploring the History of Admixture and the Genetic Basis of Pigmentation Using Autosomal and Uniparental Markers." *PLoS Genetics* (2014). Accessed September 19, 2016. doi:10.1371/journal.pgen.1004488.

Tymins, Austin. "Re-examining the Cuban Embargo." *Harvard Political Review*, December 15, 2014. Accessed September 24, 2016. http://harvardpolitics.com/world/reexamining-cuban-embargo/.

Printed in the United States
By Bookmasters